THE LOST INTERVIEWS

NEILL BIRSS

PENGUIN BOOKS

PENGUIN

UK | USA | Canada | Ireland | Australia
India | New Zealand | South Africa | China

Penguin is an imprint of the Penguin Random House group
of companies, whose addresses can be found at
global.penguinrandomhouse.com.

Penguin
Random House
New Zealand

First published by Penguin Random House New Zealand, 2016

10 9 8 7 6 5 4 3 2 1

Text © Neill Birss, 2016
Photography © as credited in captions

Cover and internal design by Sam Bunny © Penguin Random
House New Zealand, 2016
Cover photograph © Richard Menzies
Photograph on chapter openers from Shutterstock
Printed and bound in Australia by Griffin Press,
an Accredited ISO AS/NZS 14001 Environmental Management
Systems Printer

A catalogue record for this book is available from the National
Library of New Zealand.

ISBN 978-0-14-357398-2
eISBN 978-1-74-348720-4

penguin.co.nz

CONTENTS

Introduction

'I'd like to do a series of articles about the Indian Scout and get them into a magazine,' I told Burt Munro in Invercargill in the late 1960s. He jumped at the idea — publicity generated support for his trips to the United States.

Over a few months, I spent evenings at the modest garage in which he lived. I typed notes on my Olympia portable typewriter as we talked. I took them in the first person — the words just as Burt spoke them. His speech was pretty typical of a southern New Zealander of his age, a slight Southland burr derived from the early Scots settlers and pronunciation closer to Australian than present-day New Zealand speech. When Burt was a boy, a regular shipping service linked Southland with Tasmania, and people moved between the two places. I suspect the clacking typewriter sometimes caused Burt to speak more formally than usual.

We drank many cups of tea, the water scooped from a big drum outside the garage. He cooled metal in the drum, but the tea still tasted fine. Burt was fairly deaf. Sometimes he wouldn't hear a question, or would mishear it, or would hear some of it but not all. He would cup a hand behind an ear, lean forward and say, 'What was that, Neill?' or more often, 'Whazzat?'

Burt slept in the cool, damp corner of the concrete-block, flat-roofed garage. His Indian and Velocette motorcycles shared the dry corner. The shed looked like the workshop it was. You sniffed oil, metal, and tyre rubber. He wore cheap, off-the-shelf reading glasses of varying strengths, matching them to engineering tasks.

Burt was a hero in Southland long before Hollywood found him. There was a local rhyme a driver would sometimes mutter to passengers as a car got under way: 'And away we go, says Burt Munro.' When Burt built a gas device for his motorbike during World War II petrol rationing, it had two speeds — flat out and off. A south Invercargill school warned pupils to take special care if they were out around the time Burt was going to or from work.

Reading the interview notes half a century later, I better understand why Burt loved America, particularly the West. Burt came from another recently frontier society. When Burt was young, at times he worked in the bush, clearing forest for what was to become the rolling green farmland of Southland. He came from a hard-working, self-reliant people with a give-it-a-go spirit. They would likely have been as much at home in the pioneer country of the United States West.

Burt seemed to know everyone in Southland. When I first

met him, he said: 'You would be Les's son.' He explained how he and my father had worked together as bushmen [lumberjacks]. That must have been nearly half a century earlier. My only experience with motorbikes was riding an army surplus Indian around a brother-in-law's farm. Pressure on teenage city boys not to buy a motorbike was heavy. In those days of poorer roads, weak street lighting, no crash helmets, and less sophisticated medical treatment, motorcyclists were frequently killed. Some parents called motorbikes flying tombstones. When a girl mentioned a boy had invited her out, 'Does he have a motorbike?' was typically Mum and Dad's first question. 'You get a motorbike, and you can't live here,' my father successfully bluffed me. He rode an Indian when he was young. He came off on a gravel road one night. The leather helmets they wore in those days were no protection, and he was still unconscious when a motorist found him.

My lack of motorcycle experience didn't bother Burt. Patient and courteous, he would explain details, if need be, repeatedly. He would occasionally fire up the Velocette outside, with its colossal roar. We took it to the beach for a run, where the Velocette seized up soon after starting. 'Blow-ups' were milestones of Burt's engineering life. I remember being surprised when he told me that one of his early moulds for pistons was the can that baking powder came in. 'The Edmonds can was just the right size,' Burt said. A workmate of mine had a new Honda motorbike. I asked Burt what he thought of the Japanese motorcycles that were sweeping into the market. 'I had a look at one. You'd think it was made by watchmakers,' he said.

Burt liked women, and liked them right to the end of his life. I lived in a flat at the back of a hairdressing salon. Burt sometimes dropped in. He was likely dressed for the kill with his American bolo, or shoestring tie, and if a young hairdresser answered when he went to the wrong door he would pounce, whip a cord around her, pull her close, and joke about her waist measurement. The young woman would brush Burt away and laugh off the incident. Times have changed.

As others have noted, Burt didn't speak badly of people. He ignored slights. At times Burt raised eyebrows because he didn't hesitate to ask for something — from the use of a workshop or tools, to petrol for his car. Burt's obsession with his Indian and Velocette motorcycles was so strong that he lived on the smell of a motorcycle-oil rag, hoarding his pension and nursing his savings from the 1940s. His speed crusades required him to take the Indian to the Bonneville Salt Flats. Burt liked to tour in the US, too, driving an old car that often had to be repaired as he moved, and usually sleeping in it. Irving Hayes, an Invercargill businessman, car-racing enthusiast and friend, paid for Burt's cross-Pacific voyages, but Burt still had to scrimp and save. If Burt hinted or asked for 'a drop' of fuel or some other favour, it was more for the fastest Indian Scout's cause than for his own.

The goal of a series of articles grew until it looked as if I might have to make a small book. We got to 1969, when changes in my life halted the project. I got married, and interviewed Ron Walker, my schoolteacher when I was aged seven, for the newspaper I worked for. Now with the University of Otago, Ron turned the tables in the interview, which was supposed to be about setting up a university outpost in Invercargill. How did I do in high school? 'More or less dropped out,' I mumbled. Ron persuaded me to give education another go. Ron sent me back to school. Soon I was enrolled in correspondence courses and night classes.

Interviews with Burt should have resumed upon his return from America, but I moved to Christchurch and a night job that allowed me to continue my education by day. For a few years, life seemed to be work, study, sleep. The plan to write slabs of articles about Burt Munro for foreign motorbike magazines was postponed, delayed, delayed again, then filed in the dustbin of failed bright ideas. In the move or soon after, I lost the manuscript. Years later, after Burt's death, when George Begg was writing his book, *Burt Munro: Indian Legend of Speed*, a person both George and I knew asked me about the interviews. Burt must have mentioned them to George. I searched, but couldn't find the notes, and concluded they were lost for ever.

Decades later, at 4.35 in the morning on 4 September 2010, a magnitude 7.1 earthquake, sounding like a steam train coming down the street, rattled our house in Burnside, Christchurch. My wife Olive and I bolted from bed as things crashed around us, and sheltered under a table with our Staffordshire bull terrier. When the shaking stopped, neighbours were soon calling out to see whether we oldsters were alive and unhurt. We were, but all around there were fallen chimneys and fences, and inside our home was a mess.

Then, on 22 February 2011 a magnitude 6.3 quake, only 5 kilometres under the surface, struck the city at lunchtime. It flattened much of the central business district, killing 185 people. Power, water and sewerage were cut, and like scores of thousands of others, we worried about our grandchildren at school and their parents at work in the city centre. Over the next two years, thousands of aftershocks followed, including 54 over magnitude 5.

Our suburb was lucky, being built on the gravel of an old riverbed. Our house was still standing but the roof needed repairing twice, and inside things needed patching up. It was about three years before repairers could come. To make room, we shifted as much as we could into the garage. What we couldn't squeeze in, we threw away. As I dumped old university notes in a rubbish skip, a faded red folder of the kind I had kept lecture notes in fell open. The notes were typed on plain paper rather than in my usual handwritten scrawl on ruled sheets. I glanced at the first sentences. It was the Burt Munro interviews.

So here they are. Burt's story was well told in Roger Donaldson's video documentary, followed by his great feature film, and then in a graphic 'scrapbook' of Burt's life. George Begg earlier gave a good engineering and bike-racing perspective.

Tim Hanna has written about Burt, too. As I reviewed the notes, I talked to motorcycling veterans and recognised one aspect of Burt I took for granted. He wasn't a tall man and he was lean. Being light was important for racing motorcyclists. Burt was built for the Indian Scout Munro Special.

I hope this account, in Burt's words, fleshes out some details of Burt's great story.

Join us in the Munro shack. Sit back on a wooden chair with a cup of Munro tea. Savour the smell of oil and fuel. Burt's in full cry, his usually soft Southland voice now loud. With his poor hearing, he doesn't notice the clacking of the typewriter as I race to keep up with him. If we're lucky, Burt will give us a break (but not the neighbours) by taking us outside and revving up the Velocette.

Note

Then, as now, I take notes as the interviewee says them — this builds a mine of direct quotes to pop into stories. Here, I've left the notes of the Burt Munro interviews in the first person. It will be as though Burt is speaking to you, the reader. I've rejigged some notes into sentences, and I've backgrounded Burt's words with my commentary, which is set within square brackets. Otherwise, you are pretty much listening to Burt.

Neill Birss, December 2015

Notes about this book

1. Herbert James Munro was known in Southland as Bert. Here I call him Burt, the American spelling he came to prefer. 'Bert' was someone's choice, however, for his gravestone.
2. Burt died on 6 January 1978, aged 78, of natural causes. Burt is speaking in this book in the late 1960s.
3. The second main character in this story is the 1920 Indian Scout motorcycle. The model was launched on the market in October 1919, a 606-cc (37 cubic inch) V-twin. The designer, Charles B. Franklin, was educated in his native Dublin as an electrical engineer. He raced motorcycles, and in 1905, as a member of the British national team, was the first Irish motorcyclist to race internationally. He competed in the second Isle of Man TT (Tourist Trophy) and in the next six. He rode an Indian in the event in 1910, and went to work for the Indian company in 1914. Around this time, Indian Motocycle Company became the world's biggest manufacturer of motorcycles. Burt bought a second Indian Scout, a 1924 model, when he went to Australia in the 1920s. He brought this back to New Zealand, but later sold the engine.
4. The original Indian Motocycle Company didn't have an 'r' in its name.
5. Burt uses several names for the Bonneville Salt Flats in north-western Utah, where he made his record-attempt runs on the Indian motorcycle: Bonneville, Salt Lake, the Salt, the Salt Flats, the Salt Flat, the Lake, and even Wendover, which is the town on the edge of the Bonneville Salt Flats. Racing takes place at part of the Bonneville Salt Flats sometimes known as the Bonneville Speedway.
6. The record attempts are held at Bonneville in mid-August during what is known as Speed Week. Sometimes Burt called it Hot Rod Week, or Hot Rod Speed Week. After a successful qualifying run, two flying mile runs are averaged.

The American Motorcyclist Association issues the records. Classes vary with capacity, with streamlining or the absence thereof, with frame, whether the bike is a production model, and even with fuel used. The rules for streamliner class changed just ahead of Burt's last visit to Bonneville. Cars and motorcycles on sponsored attempts have booked times for runs at Bonneville after Speed Week, and Burt sometimes was invited to run during these time slots.

7. Burt often referred to bikes as 'she'. In tune with the times, he talked of 'salesmen' rather than 'salespeople'.

8. I've changed to 'African-American' Burt's original 'Negro', but in places I've left many American words, such as 'gas' for fuel. New Zealanders say 'petrol' for fuel. They also say 'sheep station' for 'sheep ranch', and 'skip' for 'dumpster'. A 'ute', or 'utility', is a pick-up vehicle in America. Kerosene in some countries is called paraffin. There are other American–British English differences in car terms most people know: boot — trunk; hood — bonnet; windshield — windscreen. Burt moves between them all.

9. In currency, I've used US dollars for the purchase of cars for Burt's travels in America and for other expenses there. Otherwise, unless otherwise specified, the dollars are New Zealand dollars or, in earlier years, New Zealand pounds. New Zealand adopted decimal currency in 1967. From then to February 2014, purchasing power of the dollar has declined by — well, that would be a guess. One pound in 1929 when Burt Munro was returning from Australia very roughly would likely buy 50 times what the equivalent two dollars would buy in early 2015.

10. New Zealand changed to metric measurements in December 1976. At the risk of interrupting narrative flow, I've inserted metric equivalents where needed. Conversion is complicated by different US and imperial (British) non-metric measurements. For example, the US gallon is equivalent to 3.785 litres, while the imperial gallon was

4.546 litres. A US, or short, ton is 0.907 metric tons. I haven't offered conversions of the three-mile sections of the Salt Flats trials.

11. In Burt's sawmilling days, assistant breaker, fiddler and shoeman were timber-mill occupations. A bushman was a woodsman or forester.

12. The beech, or sometimes birch, trees Burt talks of in his early days working in the bush is silver beech (*Nothofagus menziesii*), a hardwood tree common in southern New Zealand.

13. The American Motorcycle Association, or AMA, which issued Burt with his speed records at Bonneville, in 1976 changed its name to the American Motorcyclist Association. Burt Munro was added to its Hall of Fame in 2006. The world's largest motorcycling association, the AMA represents more than 200,000 American riders.

For visitors to Southland

Southland is the southernmost region in New Zealand. It is at the southern tip of one of the world's most remote countries. Here, you are below 46 degrees south, which puts you in the notorious Roaring Forties, north of the Furious Fifties. If you go to the Oreti Beach motorcycle racing, the sea, beyond a few nearby islands, is the Great Southern Ocean, sometimes known as the Antarctic Ocean.

When Burt was born, Southland was on the very southern fringe of the then British Empire. Most of the people descend from Scots pioneers, who turned bush into rich, green farmland. In Southland, and beside it, were goldfields, and miners moved to and from Australia and California. Burt, when a salesman, sold motorcycles to men still mining for gold. One of the early-days characters of these goldfields was an American, Bully Hayes, whose other careers included kidnapping Pacific Islanders and selling them as slave labour. He was reputed to be the last American pirate, though he took over ships by trickery rather than by force. Dutch Pete, the cook on Hayes' ship, killed him in 1877.

If you go to the hill-climb event on Bluff Hill you are beside the harbour where about two centuries ago whalers called. New Zealand now opposes whaling, but the sea classic, Frank Bullen's *The Cruise of the Cachalot*, tells of Nantucket and other whalers visiting Bluff as they hunted what they called the Solander whaling grounds south of the South Island. Bluff was the base of a famous local whaler, Paddy Gilroy, and his ship, the *Chance*. Bullen called Gilroy 'a king of men'.

This southern coast was one of the earliest parts of New Zealand settled by Europeans — whalers, sealers and adventurers — before the farming migrants arrived. From the beginning, the European arrivals intermarried with local Maori. Their famous chief, Tuhawaiki, came to lead his people in most of the South Island. The whalers called him Bloody Jack, not because of his undoubted warrior prowess, but because of the swear word he picked up from the whalers.

Invercargill has an unusual liquor sales system you will likely encounter if you visit. In 1905, Invercargill voted for local prohibition — alcohol sales were banned. This continued until 1945, when returning soldiers successfully tipped the vote and ended the drought. It never had been fully effective. During prohibition, a hotel not far from the city boasted the longest bar south of the Equator and, because breweries were allowed to stay on, it was said you could buy a keg of beer though you couldn't buy a glass of it.

When prohibition ended, citizens voted for the first of the country's licensing trusts. The Invercargill Licensing Trust has a monopoly on takeaway liquor sales and runs hotels. It ploughs profits back into the city: swimming pools, a cycling velodrome and a sports stadium. The Trust, as locals call it, also distributes about $10 million a year to local community and sports organisations. Opinions on the Trust vary, but if you have a drink in Invercargill you will probably be its customer.

Other New Zealanders will likely draw your attention to Southlanders' speech. Its most obvious difference from other New Zealand and Australian speech is the burred 'r', especially noticeable before consonants, as in 'Bur-r-r-t', our subject.

Chapter 1
THE EARLY YEARS

[Herbert James (Burt) Munro was born in Invercargill on 25 March 1899. His grandfather came to New Zealand from the north of Scotland. At age 18, he landed in Dunedin, and walked the 132 miles (220 km) to Invercargill and took a farm, Gladfield, near Mokotua, in Southland. Burt's father, William, also a farmer, was born in New Zealand. William married Burt's mother, Lily Agnes Robinson, in 1896.]

There wasn't much joy when I was born. My twin sister died at birth and Dr Ewart told my mother that I wouldn't live to reach my second birthday. But I grew into a normal, healthy child on the family farm, which was then at Morton Mains, also in Southland.

When I was two, and supposed to have been dead, I can

remember creeping along a brick path on the farm and going eeling with my father. Shortly before, just before my memory begins, I was knocked out for the first time in my life. My mother put me on a high bed and propped me up with pillows so I wouldn't fall, but somehow I got over them and crashed to the floor. She rushed in and found me unconscious on the floor with blood pouring from my head. My mother, who was then only 24, told me years later that she wrapped me in a shawl and ran with me across the paddocks to where my father was ploughing behind a team of horses.

'Oh, Willie!' she cried to my father. 'Burt's dead.'

She pulled back the shawl, and there I was laughing. I've been knocked out dozens of times since then but that's the only time I came out of it laughing.

When I was two, my father bought another farm, called Gladfield, at Mokotua, also in Southland. This was the very farm his father, an immigrant from the north of Scotland, had taken when he walked more than 100 miles [160 km] to Invercargill from Dunedin, many years before. We didn't stay there long until we moved again. This time to a farm at Asher's Siding, near Gorge Road. Asher had been a big sawmiller, and the farm was mostly stumps and rushes. About this time, I started school. I remember being reprimanded at the Asher's school for gazing out the window instead of paying attention to the blackboard.

It was only a matter of months before we were on the move again, and my father became manager of the Elston Lea farm, on the southern boundary of Invercargill. My mother, Lily, or Lillian, named the farm Elston Lea after a place in a book she had read. I went to South School. The first thing I remember is a fist fight with Jack Withington, who was later gassed in World War I, and was a semi-invalid afterwards. I was never top of the class, and never bottom — just an average pupil. I did potter round with mechanical things, though, and my classmates dubbed me 'the inventor'.

By the time I was eight, I had to get up with my brother at

3.45 a.m. every day and help milk the cows. Before I left school, I could hand-milk eight cows an hour.

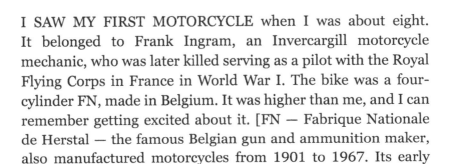

I SAW MY FIRST MOTORCYCLE when I was about eight. It belonged to Frank Ingram, an Invercargill motorcycle mechanic, who was later killed serving as a pilot with the Royal Flying Corps in France in World War I. The bike was a four-cylinder FN, made in Belgium. It was higher than me, and I can remember getting excited about it. [FN — Fabrique Nationale de Herstal — the famous Belgian gun and ammunition maker, also manufactured motorcycles from 1901 to 1967. Its early motorcycles were known for their shaft drives.]

I made a lot of little things in my spare time. These included two or three model submarines, long and shallow with a glass window in the top. They were watertight, and just heavy enough to float below the surface with their periscopes sticking out of the water. I graduated to making billy carts [in some countries called soap-box cars], a dam and waterwheel in a ditch, windmills that pumped water, and then steam turbines. I was always fond of steam.

One of my steam engines had a boiler sunk in a hole in the ground. It was raining and hailing and I was flat out stoking up the boiler, made out of an old five-gallon drum. It was bad weather, and Dad was cleaning our first car, which we had had for a little while. Mum was baking scones, and I took a spell to go and get one buttered hot. Just as I began eating it there was an explosion in the shed. My engine had exploded. It had no safety valve on it. When I wanted to lower the pressure I had to let the turbine run, but this time the pressure sneaked up while I was away. Mum and I rushed to the back door. My father came running flat out from the car shed. He thought I had been blown to bits. Did he tell me off! But my parents were understanding and tolerated my experiments. They didn't discourage me.

One of my favourite toys was a kauri yacht about three feet [90 cm] long. An old sailor had carved it out with gougers. It was fully rigged. The farm flooded quite frequently in places and when this happened I took my yacht out after cow time, and sailed it round in the floodwater. I left the yacht out in a pond one day and went to school. I and my brother, Ernie, then 13 and about 14 months older than me, decided to look for it after we finished helping milk the 35 cows that night. I wasn't allowed to go with him straight away because I had to get a pair of shoes from my sister, Eva, and take them to an aunt. Ernie went looking for the yacht by himself.

At Boundary Road, an uncle of ours, a Tasmanian bushman, was helping some people take down trees. He was cutting the roots and letting the weight of the trees bring the trunks down. The last tree of the night proved a bit of a problem and he decided to leave it to the morning. A group of young men were trying to finish the job for him when Ernie arrived looking for the yacht. He joined them in their efforts, and climbed the tree and started tugging at branches intertwined with other trees. Suddenly the tree came free, spun round, and fell to the ground, pinning Ernie underneath.

I was walking along the road when my school friend, Jack Withington, rushed out and yelled to me, 'I think Ernie's dead!' I ran into the trees, and there he was, doubled up under the tree, unconscious. I could see his face going black. Jack ran for my uncle, and he arrived with neighbours. They got Ernie out, but too late. He was dead.

I cried for days, and it was nearly 12 years before I could bring myself to visit his grave.

[Apart from his unnamed twin sister, who died at birth, and brother, Ernest, who was killed in this accident in 1912, Burt had four sisters — Ruby, Florence, Evelyn and Rita — and a younger brother, Charles. Florence, about five years younger than Burt, became a novelist, Florence Preston. Burt also had an adopted brother, John, usually known by his initials J.B. — for John Baldwin Munro. After raising their family of six surviving children, Burt's mother and father were foster parents to seven state-ward children. J.B. was the youngest. He had suffered polio and spent months in hospital in Dunedin after corrective surgery. When he was about eight and the last of the Munros' foster children, the welfare authorities (in those days, the Child Welfare Division of the Education Department) moved to take J.B. from the family. They regarded Mr and Mrs Munro as too old to continue being foster parents. The Munros fought the system. They consulted the young J.B. and, when he agreed, adopted him, and so he remained in the family. J.B. was Labour Member of Parliament for Invercargill from 1972 to 1975, and for 20 years was chief of IHC, the New Zealand organisation for supporting intellectually disabled children. He did international work for disabled people, and much other charitable work within New Zealand.]

WHEN WE FIRST CAME TO Invercargill, my father took me past a tinsmith where the Southland Building Society office now stands in Tay Street. There was a drop of eight feet or 10 feet [2.4 to 3.1 metres] to the footpath. Then later we went to a fellow Hatch, in Tweed Street, where muttonbirds were melted down. They used a suction gas engine. I remember quite well seeing it running. It was a big stationary engine. Later, my father and I used to take dray-loads of chaff to the man.

[Joseph Hatch (born 1837, died 1928), Mayor of Invercargill, then its Member of Parliament, and a founding member of the local Chamber of Commerce and the Invercargill Fire Brigade, was a notorious entrepreneur and a controversial politician.

He is remembered most for his ruthless plundering of wildlife in the sub-Antarctic, and the loss of a supply steamer with all hands. Hatch's business, later based in Tasmania, is said to have melted down for oil at Macquarie Island up to two million penguins, plus elephant seals. There were dark horror stories alleging Hatch's men herded the birds alive into melt-down cauldrons. The muttonbirds Burt spoke of are sea birds of the petrel family. For two months each year, Stewart Island Maori harvest the chicks.]

WHEN I LEFT SOUTH SCHOOL after gaining the old Proficiency qualification at age 12 [an examination that, until 1936, children could sit in a group of subjects in standard six, or year eight, at primary school], I went to Southland Technical College night classes at the behest of my mother and learned a lot of, to me, useless things, including wood carving and how to play the mandolin harp [a type of fretless zither]. I began being paid for my work on the farm — a shilling [10 cents] a week. This was my farm labourer's wage until I was 20.

In 1915, Dad leased out Elston Lea, and we moved to a farm, Pine Grove, at Edendale. I walked every step of 14 miles to the new home beside a spring cart loaded with furniture. [From Invercargill to Edendale by road is 23 miles, or 28.6 kilometres.] At the new property I had lots of time to fiddle round making things. I was happy.

War hysteria permeated the country during World War I, and was the driving force of my first project. From newspaper headlines, we all thought Germans were about to land in New Zealand. We worked on the farm all morning, then took an hour's break for lunch. I began going into the bush and working on a cannon I thought would blast the hell out of any 'Huns' who tried to take our farm. Dad would give me a yell from the yard when lunch was over, and I would return to work.

One day he sneaked up on me and saw the project. He realised why I was so secretive about it — I was using his good fencing wire. For the barrel, I had a steel tube about four feet [1.2 metres] long. To fill in the breech I hacked the end off old spears that were used for driving pipes into the ground for well making. With a brace, I drilled quarter-inch [0.64-cm] holes in the pipe at the end of the breech. I drove a rod in tight and put a nut on the end. I used this to hold the layers of No. 8 fencing wire wound round the two-inch [5-cm] pipe for reinforcing. I drilled a touch hole — and I had a two-pounder [0.9-kg] cannon. The next step was to test it.

Harry Rodgers, a neighbour's farmhand, took a keen interest in the project and joined the gun crew for the test firing after I had finished building a three-wheel carriage that both took the recoil and enabled the weapon to be elevated or depressed. I also made a shell. This comprised a piece of pipe that fitted into the barrel with a piece of blue-gum timber in it and packed with old bolts and bits of wire. The charge was blasting powder.

All was tamped, we trained the cannon on a packing case, lit the fuse, and ran in case the barrel exploded. Boom! The packing case disintegrated, and the shell carried straight on and through the weatherboarding of the new implement shed then smashed a piece off the turnip drill.

Harry and I were thrilled. We had one more test fire. Dad had told me to shoot an old, ailing cattle dog, Fly. We took the cannon up to the 50-acre paddock to shoot old Fly. We loaded the cannon up and tied the dog to a peg. We executed him with the cannon. Dad was wild, but it was just as quick and no more painful than a rifle bullet.

'You told me to shoot the dog — you didn't say how,' I told him.

After this, Harry and I hid the cannon in a tongue of bush near the homestead and kept it trained on the front gate. We kept her fully loaded so that we would just have to light the fuse when the Germans came.

About 1940, I recovered the cannon, and the Home Guard [wartime militia] at Oteramika used it for gun-laying training, but the silly bastards never learned how to fire it. It could fire about two pounds [0.9 kg] of bolts. About 1960, the police were warning people about keeping firearms. Two policemen came to the farm, hauled the cannon away and buried it.

[Roger Donaldson's book, *The World's Fastest Indian*, has a picture of Burt with the cannon barrel. The caption says it was taken before it was surrendered to the police.]

WHEN THE FIRST SUMMER ARRIVED, I built a tree house with a 22-foot [6.7-metre] access ladder and roofed with split-open kerosene cans. I had a bed, a gramophone and a stove. Soon I was spending more nights in it than at home. On the roof I erected a signal lamp so my friend across the paddocks could make contact at night. I worked the light with a cord, and looked out from the hut for his light.

On our farm was a 10-acre [4-hectare] grass paddock dotted with black pines. Local people had long used it as a picnic ground. As added attractions, we added a merry-go-round [carousel], a see-saw and an aerial tramway. This was a single strand of No. 8 wire from treetop down to the grass. You climbed the tree by ladder, sat in a little chair hooked on to the wire by wheels, and pushed off. The wire sagged near the end, so you sat with your feet out so you could slide to rest and brake along the grass.

For someone with a mechanical bent, those were exciting days. Aeroplanes, cars and motorcycles were new contraptions and it seemed that everyone dreamed of making one for themselves. I remember seeing pioneer pilot Captain Scotland fly over Invercargill in an ancient machine. This was before we moved to Edendale. Getting enough money to buy a plane was out of the question, so there was only one thing to do — make one.

[On 20 February 1914, James William Humphrys Scotland, in his Caudron biplane, flew from Invercargill to Gore, the first cross-country flight in New Zealand. Later, in World War I, Scotland served in the Royal Flying Corps in Persia. He was the second person in the country to gain a pilot's licence.]

I began with models, but I never achieved the stage of making one big enough to carry me — or an engine for that matter. My first model, when I was about 17, was a biplane about 10 feet [3 metres] long and with wings about 10 feet by two feet. I worked on it in the loft at night by candlelight and on Sundays, which would have upset my churchgoing parents had they known.

I carved the propeller out of a piece of gate timber, made a frame of fine wire and red pine, and lined it with white calico. It had little light wooden wheels. Propulsion was by two or three big car-tyre tubes that were wound up. I took it out for a trial and found the plane was too heavy, and the propulsion too weak for the machine to fly. So I built a smaller one, about four feet [1.2 metres] long, and with much lighter wings. It would fly for up to 100 yards [91.4 metres] and climb to 20 feet or 30 feet [6 to 9 metres], propelled by wound-up elastic.

IN 1915, I HAD MY first ride on a motorcycle. Like nearly every machine I have been on since, it broke down. My parents had gone visiting to Mataura Island [a farming area] when a bunch of relatives turned up for dinner. I went across to a neighbour to borrow his old Douglas motorcycle so I could fetch them. He loaned me the bike and showed me how to work it, but forgot to tell me that every few miles oil had to be pumped into it by its hand pump. I got halfway to Mataura Island when the Douglas seized up. After it cooled, it started but ran only a short way before it seized up again.

I eventually got to Mataura Island and gave my parents the message. They set off to the farm by car and I began battling back on the old Douglas twin. The distance between seizures shortened as the journey wore on, and the time to cool grew longer. I must have pushed the machine further than I rode it. I had three miles [4.8 km] to go when the owner arrived. He had been out looking for me.

'I forgot to tell you about the oil,' he apologised.

After that, I rode the bike frequently.

LIFE ON THE FARM WAS mainly work, making things in my spare time, eating and sleeping. During the nine months of the year when the cows were in milk, I took the milk to the factory every morning in a horse-drawn spring cart. I carried a rifle in the cart to shoot rabbits. I gutted and cleaned those I shot, and sold the skins for four pence [four cents] each. This was good pocket money when wages were only a shilling a week.

I remember the flu epidemic that swept the world and arrived in New Zealand in 1918. In the nearby tiny township of Wyndham, about 25 victims were buried in one day. Many people who survived were too ill to work for weeks. I can remember for a time milking 80 cows at home with machines, then milking 60 cows for a neighbour. He and his family were all down with the sickness, and I didn't see them at all while I was milking their herd.

[The 1918 influenza pandemic killed about 50 million people round the world, including 8500 in New Zealand. Southland had one of the country's highest regional death rates from it.]

After milking both herds, I took the milk to the dairy factory and spent the rest of the day making cheese. I did the work long enough to be knocked out by an 80-pound [36.3-kg] cheese that I was lifting onto a shelf. I slipped and fell across a pipe. The cheese came down and knocked me out.

I also had an accident at home about this time while I was on Dobbin, a farm hack that had been bred as a racehorse but didn't grow big enough. It was a Sunday morning, and I was sent out after breakfast to bring in some cattle. Dobbin put its foot into a rabbit burrow, and I woke up in a bed at home that evening. Everyone was out milking, so I got up and went down and gave them a hand. I think we were a harder breed in those days.

———————————————35———————————————

IN THE WINTER OF 1919, I left Southland for a few months and went north. Dad had sold the Edendale farm and moved back to Elston Lea. I took advantage of the winter break from milking, and with a friend, Dick Peterson, decided to have a look at the 'big smoke' — Christchurch. We had a great time, and were broke in a couple of weeks. Dick's people lived around Akaroa, and he wanted me to go cocksfoot-grass cutting with him to earn some money, but I was sick of the sight of farms. Instead, I went to Otira, where I heard they were looking for men to work in the railway tunnel, which when finished would link the West Coast with Canterbury.

I had enough money for the train trip from Christchurch to Arthur's Pass, but not enough to ride in the old horse-and-coach over the pass, so I walked through snow up to two feet

[0.6 metres] deep. An old fellow, wheeling a bicycle, was going through, too. He wasn't very fit, and I ended up pushing the bike for him. It was bleak, and the sight of two horses lying dead in the river where there had been a coach accident made me wonder what was ahead for me.

The five shillings I had in my pocket just covered a night's lodging at the hotel at Otira. I got a job on tunnel construction the next day. They gave me a hut to sleep in. The first night I lit a fire to keep out the cold, for I had no blankets. There was about 40 degrees of frost [minus 22 degrees Celsius] and every time the fire died down, the cold woke me up.

At breakfast in the morning I sat in the cookshop alongside a fellow called John Jackson who told me to go down and see Joe Serati, an old fellow who had a store halfway down Otira, and he would give me blankets on credit. He did, too.

That night with the blankets and a mattress improvised from a bag of chaff, I slept the night through. In the morning, I started work as a shovel hand. It took the gang an hour to walk through the wet tunnel until we reached the workplace. Then for six hours I shovelled concrete from the ground up over wooden boxing 11 feet [3.35 metres] high. We stood on a tray two feet [0.6 metres] off the ground. This reduced the lift to nine feet [2.74 metres], but it was still heavy work. At the end of the day we trudged back through the tunnel, water dripping and running from the roof. By the time I reached open air, the freezing cold had begun icing up my water-soaked clothes.

It was a rough life, but I stuck it through the bitter winter and into the early spring. The pay of 18 shillings a day seemed to me a fortune after my income of a shilling a week on the farm. The wetness and the cold were the things that made it so rough, not the hard work. We would wear out a pair of oilskins in a week.

Things became easier when they transferred me to the timber gang, helping put up boxing. Then I received a letter from my father telling me to 'come home at once'. He had bought another farm, this time at Fortrose, and needed my help.

ONE OF THE FIRST THINGS I did when I got back to Invercargill was buy myself a motorcycle. It cost me 50 pounds [$100] and was war surplus. It had been a machine-gun carrier overseas. An English-made Clyno V-twin, she sent spasms of pride shooting up my back as I roared home to the Fortrose farm at 55 miles an hour [88.5 km/h].

[Clyno Engineering made motorcycles and cars in Britain from 1909 to 1929, when it went into receivership, after losing a price war with Morris. At one time Clyno was Britain's third biggest car maker.]

After a summer and autumn working on the new farm, I got another winter job, this time at a sawmill at Taihaka in Western Southland's Longwood ranges. Before time came to go back to the cows, I helped to break down a million feet of birch as an assistant breaker, then as a fiddler in the pit. As a fiddler, my workmates and I cut down to ordered size about eight trolley-loads of logs a day. Sawing into the hard beech was much tougher than working in the tunnel. I saved my money, then went back to the cows.

By this time, my itchy-footed father had sold his Fortrose farm and bought another at Oporo, nearer to Invercargill. On a trip from this farm to town one day I saw an Indian motorcycle and knew I had to have one.

The next winter I worked at a sawmill at Hell's Gully, East Limehills, run by the Murihiku Sawmilling Company. I was a shoeman, hauling logs from a trolley onto a bank. Then I took a contract lifting old tramway for five shillings a chain [22 yards, or 20.1 metres]. I was able to lift six chains of sleepers a day, and saved five pounds a week. By milking season, I had enough money to buy myself a 1920 Indian Scout, with an acetylene headlamp. I couldn't afford 10 pounds for the model with an electric headlight.

I kept my treasured bike in the hay barn. Its main use was transport to dances at the weekend. Fred Finlayson, who worked on a neighbouring farm, used to come with me as pillion passenger. When I got home at 2 a.m., I polished the Indian until she looked new again. Then I went to bed.

It wasn't long before I had my first spill. My uncle Alf was a motorcyclist, too. He and I rode down to Kapuka to visit my grandmother. We were about to leave in the morning. I was sitting impatiently on my Indian while Alf battled to start his King Dick twin. He was still kicking her after about five minutes, and I thought I would try to pass the time by trying to ride the Indian while standing in the saddle. It was a stupid thing to do. I controlled her in the gravel up to about 15 miles an hour [24 km/h]. Then, crash! I regained consciousness that night.

Bikes then weren't meant to do much more than 30 miles per hour [48.3 km/h]. Their iron pistons would get very hot if you rode much over that.

Not long after, about 1921 or 1922, I had my first motorcycle race. It was on Oreti Beach, which for years has been the hub of two-wheel racing sport in Southland and only lately has gone out of use because of erosion of sand. [Burt was talking in the 1960s; it has been in use since then.] I raced Bert Collett, who had a 7.9 Indian, twice the size of my machine. We went right down to the river. Bert had the speed, but mine was lighter, and while he slowed to go around kelp lying on the beach, I just bounced over the top of it. I won.

From 1921, I took a job as a carpenter in Invercargill but still kept on milking the cows to pay my board at Elston Lea, where the family had returned. Just before this I had spent a few months working in a bush camp where we cut slabs of manuka to be sold for firewood. We slept in tents on manuka scrub mattresses. They were a good bunch of workmates, but some were pretty tough. I remember one of them was an Australian Aborigine, Tom Stott, who had been in trouble a few years earlier for shooting up a house in Edendale after he had been jilted by a farm girl.

Riding through the swamp to the camp was my first taste of motocross. It was pretty tough on the bike. I used to maintain her myself, and sometimes I would pull her down after work, grind the valves by kerosene light and have her running again by midnight.

Motorcycle fever had me well and truly by then, and I would go anywhere at the drop of a hat just to be riding the Indian. In those days, you raced everyone you met on the road. There were a few hazards you don't meet today — like horses. I took at least one spill on the gravel because of them, and broke my ankle, too.

In Invercargill at this time there was a big roller-skating rink, King's Hall, which the locals claimed to be the best in the world, and they claimed to have the world speed-skating champion to go with it. He was a fellow Lyons, and he was certainly far faster than any of the other Southland skaters. They asked me to race him on my motorcycle and I agreed. I was pacing him round the floor when I smashed into the fence and broke the engine lug on the crankcase, though I wasn't hurt, apart from a few bruises.

GETTING ROUND ON MY MOTORCYCLE made me curious to see what the rest of the world was like, and I decided to start off by taking my bike up through the North Island — a big adventure in those days. Travelling on the main roads was like cross-country riding today. It was just about as rough.

The trip as far north as the Kaikouras [twin mountain ranges in the north-east of the South Island] was uneventful, but in that area I had a nasty fright, and felt the actual pain of fear, like an iron band on the chest, for the first time in my life.

I was belting up the road, bound for Blenheim, and came over a hill. On one side of the road was a man scything grass. Suddenly, from the other side, a cow leaped out and ran in front of me. I can still now see, to one side that man continuing to swing the big scythe, from the other side the cow rushing across, and me roaring towards a diminishing gap. In a fraction of a second, I was through the gap, but for what seemed minutes I could see in my mind a picture of tangled motorcycle parts, cow, human flesh and a great, bloodied scythe. The pain in my chest came afterwards and lasted for minutes.

By the time I reached Blenheim, I was out of money, or rather didn't have enough for lodging as well as petrol. I parked the Indian on the roadside and lay down in a paddock for the night. I was woken at dawn by a commotion, and found a bull's red eyes measuring me up. He was roaring and pawing the ground. I rolled under the fence, onto the road so quickly he didn't know I was gone.

I got a job carpentering in Blenheim to build up my funds. The boss offered me another two shillings a day to stay when I left, but the road was calling and I kept on. After a look around Nelson, I sailed on the ferry across Cook Strait to Wellington and began riding through the North Island.

The first call was at Feilding to see an old friend, Bondy Dewe. There I saw grass-track motorcycle racing for the first time. Bondy took me to watch Excelsior Big X, Douglas, Harley and Indian machines race on a mile [1.6-km] grass track. Some of the better riders were lapping at more than 70 miles per hour [112.6 km/h].

Later, between Napier and Rotorua, I came off the road and hurt my hand. I pressed on through the wilderness. It was near dark when I came across a gang of Maori knapping stones to metal the then dirt road. [To 'knap' is to hammer or chip.] They invited me to stay the night after I asked how much further it was to Rotorua. I stayed with them, and in the morning they took me to a sulphur spring, where I bathed my hand for half an hour — until I could open and close it. They gave me breakfast, then I was on my way.

In Rotorua, they were charging four shillings a gallon for petrol, and that was a lot of money in those days [1923]. When I complained, they explained it was because they had to transport the fuel so far from a port.

The next part of the trip was to Auckland over some shocking roads — miles and miles of clay and bush tracks, sometimes with logs lying about. The roads were so rough and potholed that the Indian toolkit in a leather portmanteau punched right through the leather and onto the road.

By the time I reached Auckland I was broke again, and had to borrow ten pounds to finance the return trip from Alex Storrie, an Invercargill implement manufacturer who had retired to Auckland.

The machine took another battering on the way south. By the time I reached Christchurch she needed new rings for her iron pistons. She started to run very hot, and I had to stop at ever shorter distances between irrigation ditches and douse her with water to cool her down. There was no compression, and she was getting weaker and weaker, until at Richmond, five miles [8 km] from Oamaru, she gave up the ghost and died. People in a railway house put me up for the night, and in the morning I pulled her apart on the side of the road, fitted rings and got her going again.

I rode through the afternoon down to Dunedin, then to Balclutha, and on through the Catlins, one of New Zealand's forgotten corners, a wild piece of beautiful coastal bushland, isolated and undeveloped while Southland and Otago have grown around it. I stayed the night with my cousin on his bush farm, and the next day I rode cross-country through bush farms and over forest tracks to pick up the main Invercargill–Dunedin road at Clinton. You couldn't get through Tokanui in those days, and I have never believed in doubling back on my tracks.

I rode through streams, up hills, through bogs, and lifted the 300-pound [136-kg] machine over fences to cut across paddocks until I made it to the main road. I reached Invercargill by one o'clock in the afternoon.

The Indian agent in Invercargill wanted me to give the story of my trip to the local newspapers. That's how awed they were about a motor journey to Auckland and back in the 1920s.

AFTER THE LONG TRIP, I worked at a number of things: as a contractor building stables and barns and even putting another storey on a house. I helped to build a new block at the Mataura paper mill, and worked for a builder in Invercargill. I hadn't served an apprenticeship, so had to go on apprentice's wages and serve my time. I got tired of this so went to work at the paper mill. I made about 12 pounds a week there, but for this I had to work about 100 hours.

I also contracted for the Southland Power Board, putting cross-arms on power poles. I lived in a hut, and we ate our meals on a table in the mud under a canopy stretched between the huts. I used to go shearing, too. I worked at Blackmount Station for about three seasons. I was the wrong build to be a gun shearer, and for me it was hard work. The best I could do with the [hand] blades was to shear 130 sheep a day. I averaged about 100. The ringer at Blackmount shed used to shear about 180 a day. ['Gun', as in 'gun shearer', is a word for champion or expert that goes back to English medieval times. 'Ringer' is the fastest shearer in a shed.]

One wet Sunday about 1921, I rode my motorcycle through the unfinished road as far as I could towards Redcliff Station, which was reached from Te Anau. When I got back to Blackmount, the station owner, a Mr McLean, said, 'In a few years you will be able to ride right through to Redcliff on your bike.' That road is now just being completed. [Nearly 50 years later.]

At all these jobs, my faithful Indian Scout was with me, parked beside my sleeping quarters. There was one place I didn't take her — that was to sea. The year after I worked in the Otira rail tunnel, I worked as a stoker on the *Waimana*, a coaster, and on the *Kamo*, which used to go to the Chatham Islands. I was a shocking sailor. I was sick for weeks on end and sweated it out down in the boiler room, where it was so hot you had to drink oatmeal and water to replace your sweat, and needed eight hours off to recover from each four-hour watch. In a following wind, I once saw the temperature climb above 140 degrees Fahrenheit [60 degrees Celsius].

I got into a fight or two. I had one scrap with a former navy boxing champion. I didn't win that one. I can remember being at Greymouth for two or three days, and failing to keep a date with a girl because I was down to only tuppence [two cents] in my pocket. Soon after this I left the sea for good.

One night I pulled the bike down, ground the valves, then went out late for a test run. I was belting along the road about 45 miles per hour [72.4 km/h] when two horses jumped out from a hedge and started to race me along the road. Just as I was about to hit them, they swerved. I hit one with my shoulder, then I crashed. I was off work for a week with a badly sprained ankle, and the horses' owner paid my wages for the week.

Chapter 2
TO AUSTRALIA

By 1924, I had also left behind for good my farmhand's wages of a shilling a week. In 1925, I married Beryl [Florence Beryl Martyn, always known as Beryl], and took my new wife to new pastures over the Tasman — Australia.

We crossed the Tasman in the *Maunganui*. We slept in different cabins. I was in a cabin of 12 men, one of whom was a vaudeville escape artist of the Great Houdini type. I don't remember much about him except that I had all my savings with me and slept with them under my pillow, frightened that 'Houdini' would spirit them away.

When we landed in Sydney, we rented a flat in Kings Cross and I went to work as a carpenter with the Sydney City Council. Neither the job nor the flat was very satisfactory so in a short time we moved to Glebe Point, a quieter area in those days, and

I was working for a private contractor who did maintenance work on big stores.

One of the first things I did in Sydney was go to the motorcycle races. I think the famous Maroubra Speedway opened that year. [It opened in December 1925 at Maroubra as the Olympia Motor Speedway.] It certainly was the first track I visited. I also went to see the Speedway Royal at the Sydney Showground, the first dirt-racing track in the world, and I went to the one-mile [1.6-km] dirt track at Penrith at the foot of the Blue Mountains.

[Burt was talking about the Speedway Royal, later called the Speedway Royale, a dirt track on the old Sydney Showground. Riders raced on it from the 1920s until the 1990s. In later years it was better known for car racing. Some sources suggest motorcyclists were racing on small dirt tracks in Australia and the United States before World War I.]

It wasn't long before I bought a 1924 Indian Scout, and I was back in business. I haunted the Maroubra track and soon became pit mechanic to Eddie Dark, a great sidecar man. He persuaded me to go in my first race, and it was a sidecar event. As passenger I had a friend, Chicker Wells. The strain of the sidecar was too much for the Indian Scout, despite the work I had been putting into her. She burned out her iron cylinders at the end of the first mile.

Eddie Dark later broke the world sidecar record. He was only one of a few great riders who performed regularly at Maroubra and the other tracks. Cars competed at Maroubra, too. I remember a millionaire called Jones who used to drive there. Jones built a hill at Lithgow with a reward of a hundred pounds [$200] to any rider who could climb it. The grade was about 45 degrees, with a huge boulder on either side and, on the crest, a tree stump which a rider had to swerve past. None of the Sydney boys could get to the top, but a famous American rider, 'Sprouts' Elder, whom I consider the greatest hill climber of all time, arrived on the scene with a side-valve, 80-inch Indian. He won a hundred pounds on his second try.

At the opening of the Casula hill climb in Sydney, which then had a grade of about one in two, Sprouts told the officials he didn't want to mess up their new slant track, and rode up the terraced bank beside it in a cloud of dirt. He was reported to be doing 60 miles per hour [96.6 km/h] when he hit the top. When Sprouts made his first ride at Maroubra, there was awe as he roared round the circuit, lapping at 97 miles per hour [156 km/h] on a 74-inch [188-cm] Indian Chief. This was as fast as the fastest of the supercharged racing cars.

[Lloyd 'Sprouts' Elder, a Californian who died in 1957, was an outstanding competitor in Britain as well as Australia. He pioneered 'broad sliding' — speedway — in the United States. Elder lost the fortune he accumulated from speedway riding in a failed mining venture, and after retiring from racing he was in the California Highway Patrol.]

My second race in Sydney was in a cross-country, known today as motocross. It was the Chatswood Miniature TT. We rode through a bush track where the Sydney suburb of Chatswood now stands. I had made a sidecar to transport my wife and our child. I left this behind, and I was off in what I believe was one of the first scrambles in the world. Cec Weatherby, an Aussie who a few months earlier had raced at the Isle of Man, and I fought it out, wheel and wheel, most of the way. There were 10 laps of the third-of-a-mile [536-metre] course, and by the last lap Weatherby had it on me, and I crossed the line second.

[In November 1928, Cec Weatherby was the first motorcyclist in Australia to top 100 mph — 161 km/h.]

IN OUR SECOND YEAR IN Sydney, I got a job helping to build the big powerhouse in Botany Bay. About 2000 men were working on the project, and I can remember Jack Lang, the Labor Premier of New South Wales, haranguing us about the benefits of socialism.

While I was working there, the American anarchists Sacco and Vanzetti were executed for an alleged murder in Massachusetts. Workers round the world thought the charges had been trumped up. I remember everyone downing tools to march on the Sydney Town Hall in protest. I was one of about a hundred and thirty who didn't march. It wasn't so much that my sympathies weren't with the marchers, as the fact that I have never been a joiner. Only a handful of the boys made it to the town hall, anyway. Every pub the demonstration passed, it lost a bit of the parade, and there was a host of pubs between Botany Bay and the town hall.

My position on the project was a pannikin boss [an Australian term for an overseer of a smallish group of workers]. In my gang I had about twenty men, and for the little extra money I got each week I was supposed to do more than my share of risky work. One job that sticks clearly in my memory is when I had to walk out on a one-foot four-inch [40.6-cm] steel girder suspended over 110 feet [33.5 metres] of daylight. I tried not to think of the daylight as I edged out and slipped a loop over the end, then turned, and marched back.

During my annual holiday from the project, I decided to take my wife and our now two children down to Canberra in the motorbike and sidecar. We decided to take the 'covered wagon' — as we called the bike and home-made sidecar — across the Blue Mountains to Goulburn, then down to the capital. We struck rotten weather. It poured all the time as the Indian battled up the mountains with the four of us. The engine grew hotter until it 'cooked' a piston a few miles before we got to Marulan, a little town with a pub, a police station, a store and a few houses. We chugged the last leg into Marulan over a gravel road and it began to snow before we arrived.

I sent the wife and family to the hotel while I pulled the cylinder off the engine. I had to go to Goulburn to get a new piston, so I got a lift with a commercial traveller who was just pulling out, and made it to Dave Brewster's motorcycle shop in Goulburn. The only thing he could find was an old BSA alloy piston. He machined the piston to suit.

Then I set about trying to get back to Marulan. I got down to the railway and found the next train didn't leave till midnight. I was worried about my family. I had told my wife to book into the hotel as I rushed off, and hadn't time to say anything else. There was nothing I could do, so I wandered around until the train left. Just before departure time I found it didn't stop at Marulan. I just had to get back to the family that night, so I chanced it and asked if I could ride in the guard's van [in America, the caboose]. They agreed, and after about 20 miles [32 km] it slowed to go through Marulan. I put the cylinder and piston under my arm and prepared to jump. There was no lighting at the little station and I was scared stiff that I would hit the points lever, but I had no alternative.

I waited till I was about level with the hotel, and jumped. I spun through the darkness for a second, then crashed on gravel and somersaulted into long grass beside the track. I had made it. Even today, 40 years since then, I dream about that jump into the darkness.

I walked over to the hotel and asked what room my family was in.

'They're not here,' the manager told me. 'We were full up when you pulled in.' He suggested the police might be able to help me find them.

I walked up to the police station in a panic. When I knocked, a big, friendly voice boomed at me to come inside. There were the policeman, his wife and my wife, a roaring fire and a table covered with supper. The children were asleep in the next room. We never forgot the hospitality of Constable Love and his wife, and for years afterwards we called on them whenever we passed.

In the morning, the weather was a little better. I fixed the bike and we rode off to Melbourne, the children in the covered wagon, and my wife on the pillion seat.

I HAD ONE OR TWO crashes in Sydney. One of the most painful, though no bones were broken, was when I was riding home to Glebe Point after working all day at Botany Bay. I was stopped by a policeman on point duty in Cleveland Street at rush hour. Just as we got the go-ahead signal a guy in a big car behind us drove forward and ran right over my leg with his front wheel. Excruciating pain shot up my thigh and I could feel the bone about to snap. He stopped dead, and stared through the windscreen, his eyes popping out.

'Back up, you bastard!' I roared.

He snapped out of his trance and considerately backed his car off me. He was driving an Australian Six, an early Australian car built like a tank. [These were made in Australia from 1919 to 1925 using imported and local parts. Most had straight-six engines from the Rutenber Motor Company of Chicago.]

It was typical of the treatment motorcyclists get from many car and truck drivers all over the world. People are always talking about motorcycles being self-propelled coffins, and consider motorcyclists suicidal maniacs, but, believe me, it's the four-wheel drivers who kill us.

The other major mishap I had in Sydney was also with an Australian Six. I was taking my wife and year-old child, June, home after a picnic at Botany Bay. I was going faster than I should have been when an Australian Six came flying out of a side street. The only way to miss him as he crossed in front of me was to turn sharp right. We missed all right, but the turn was so sharp that the bike turned right over the top of the covered-over sidecar. I jumped off before I was skewered on the road, then crawled frantically on my hands and knees, dodging the machine as it bounced end over end, with my wife and the baby, who luckily were only shaken up. The car didn't even stop.

WORK AT BOTANY BAY GROUND to a halt. There wasn't enough money to carry on with the job. It was 1928 and the Depression was just around the corner. It wasn't easy to get work. In fact, it proved so hard to find a job in Sydney that I decided to take my wife and family to Melbourne.

I called on an Indian agent soon after we arrived in the Victorian capital. I hadn't cleaned the red dust from the goat tracks they called roads when I parked outside and strolled in. In the shop, I heard that there was a hill climb on. I put my name down for it.

'What are you riding?' the agent, Frank Campbell, asked me.

'That old Scout out there,' I said, and pointed to the dust-covered Indian.

'It's no use going in with that thing,' said the shop owner. 'There are real champions riding down here.'

I went in any way and paid my 2s 6d [25 cents] entry fee. The hill climb was on a Sunday and it turned out to be the Victorian championship.

I got on the line. All the other bikes in the climb were bigger than mine. There were Big Chiefs and Super Scouts and so on, and there were remarks such as, 'What does that silly so-and-so think he's doing here with that little bike?'

But I had done my homework. My Scout had modified handlebars, bigger wheels, and I had replaced the iron pistons with alloy pistons that I bought second-hand in Sydney and modified. I had enlarged the valves, ground the backs off the cams, and fitted a Powerplus carburettor and manifold. I had bored out the barrel by putting grinding paste on old pistons and working away at home at nights. The upshot was that I surprised them all and won the state hill-climb championship.

———————————⟨35⟩———————————

I JOINED THE NORTHCOTE MOTORCYCLE Club in Melbourne and spent a lot of time at the sport. The building industry had been hit badly by a long timber strike, and I had two or three jobs with gaps of unemployment during the eight months I was in Melbourne. When I was out of work, I put all my time into my bike.

One weekend, the Northcote club took a run to Inverloch Beach, out of Melbourne, for speed trials. On the way down, Frank Campbell ran a petrol-consumption trial. I won with 116 miles per gallon [2.4 litres per 100 km]. It augured well for the weekend competitions.

The next day the Harley-Davidson Motorcycle Club took over the beach for speed trials. The officials didn't know what class to put me in, but finally decided that my flathead 596 cc would be a fair match for the 500 cc overhead-valve class.

I was racing against two pilots from the Point Cook Royal Australian Air Force Base. They were riding two-cam Harleys, supposed to be very fast machines. At the end of the day, one of them did 96 miles per hour [154.5 km/h] and won. I tied for second at 90.01 miles per hour [144.9 km/h]. There was some consternation among the spectators, and they had grounds for it. An old flathead Scout had not been left for dead by two factory pocket-valve racers.

Frank Campbell, who by this time was a firm friend of mine, was talking to a Harley man after the race. The Harley man sneered at him and said no little Scout could do the speed I had done. When Frank told me, I challenged him to a match race. Unfortunately, I got the Harley riders mixed up and challenged the pilot who had done 96 miles per hour.

We rode down the beach then rode back together until we hit the line marking the start of the measured mile. The airman jumped the tape and got the break. I got in his slipstream and held on until he beat me by only two lengths.

The race was reported in the Melbourne newspapers. I can remember a reporter's description that we made a great sight roaring out of the mist on the beach. After the publicity, motorcyclists believed mine was no ordinary Scout.

There were some adverse results from the race, though. Challenges poured in on me from all angles, including one that I couldn't break the lap record on the Motordrome's quarter-mile [0.4-km] banked track. It had been lapped at 96 miles per hour, and would have been a great test of the machine and me if I were to try to break the record. However, the fact that I had never ridden on a small track plus my responsibility as a married man with a family decided me against any record bid.

[The Motordrome was also known as the Olympic Park Speedway, the Melbourne Speedway, or the Victorian Speedway. The ground was primarily a speedway track, but also hosted football matches. It was converted from a concrete track to a dirt track in 1933. It became the Olympic Park Stadium used during the 1956 Olympic Games. Aspendale was a venue for both horse and motor racing until 1931. Motor racing continued until the 1940s.]

HOWEVER, I USED TO PRACTISE on the Aspendale speedway, a one-mile [1.6-km] dirt track. The speedway manager, after seeing me ride, approached an Indian agent, who offered me the chance of riding a brand-new Indian overhead-valve factory racer. It was the most beautiful machine I had seen. It was one of only six produced, and could do about 100 miles per hour

[161 km/h]. I was very sorely tempted to take up the offer, but once again family considerations won out.

SO I KEPT ON POTTERING around with my Scout and eventually raced her at Aspendale. I remember racing in a five-mile [8-km] handicap and coming off decidedly second best. Having a non-racing machine, I was first away. In those days we had to use hand pumps for oil, and each time as I came down the straight I steered with one hand and with the other gave two full pumps on the oil. The pressure was high, and the pump needed to be pushed hard. The longer the race, the harder the pumping became as the cold air made the oil thicker. The rough clinker-and-dirt track at Aspendale was about 50 yards [45.7 metres] wide on the bends, with a post-and-rail fence on the outside and a two-foot [0.6-metre] wide, two-inch to three-inch [5-cm to 7.6-cm] deep gutter on the inside.

I was doing more than 90 miles per hour [144.8 km/h] and was just returning my pumping hand when I hit the gutter. Automatically, my one steering hand jerked the front wheel over. Next minute I was in a slow wobble, and instead of taking the turn I snaked and broadsided towards the post-and-rails. I was still holding the lead, but eight or nine riders were bunched in behind me. It all happened in a fraction of a second. I knew I had no chance if I hit the rails, so I decided to jump. My reflexes took over. In that fraction of a second I stood up on the Indian's footboard and jumped backwards a little. I landed on my feet, but went head over heels four times. Dazed, I knew I had to get my bike off the track for the other racers' safety. Just as I dragged it to the side, they roared into the straight again.

As I lay in the ambulance room, black and blue from the soles of my feet to the rim of my crash hat, the other boys came and told me what a narrow squeak I'd had. The Victorian dirt-track champion, Reg Hay, from Tasmania, missed my head by only six inches [15 cm] they claimed, and another rider missed me by two feet [0.6 metres]. I was too sick to care. The boys helped me and my bike to the train and I got home somehow. I lay in bed for a week, then began repairing the Scout.

Working on the bike meant I couldn't use it to go to work or even to look for work. I got around this by fitting a second engine into the frame while I modified my racing engine. Working on the engine was absorbing — sometimes too absorbing. Or so I thought when one night we had visitors and I went out to the front to see them off. The bike was gone from its usual parking place. I panicked and ran around looking for it, thinking it had been stolen. My subconscious led me out the Sydney road, and there I found it parked on the roadside, sidecar attached. Then it came back to me. At lunchtime I had ridden to a dealer's to get some kerosene. I was so engrossed by the racing engine that I forgot about the bike and walked home.

THINGS WERE GETTING TOUGHER AND tougher in Melbourne as the Depression came closer. I decided I could make a better living for the family back in New Zealand, where at least they wouldn't starve.

Before we sailed from Melbourne, I had one thing to do: sell a section I had bought in Manly. I rode up to Sydney for the weekend on the Indian to finalise the sale. It was a hell trip. The road between Melbourne and Sydney was good for about 100 miles [161 km]. Outside each city it then deteriorated into something like I think the Ho Chi Minh trail through the jungle must be like. It was hot and dusty, and the February sun cooked my forehead between the top of the goggles and my leather helmet.

I made it to Sydney and sold the land for the same price I paid for it. I never have believed in speculating on land — I think it's morally wrong. Then I headed back down the Melbourne road. Just after I reached the end of the really rough road and was on the last stretch, the lower frame bar of the bike broke. I scratched my head for a while and decided that, after so nearly finishing the trip, it wasn't going to beat me. I borrowed some clothesline from a farmhouse, lashed the frame together, and finished the ride. It was my hardest so far. I covered 200 miles [322 km] in 30 hours. I had 60 pounds [413.7 kPa] of air pressure in the tyres to stop the rims being bashed in. That saved the rims, but my new back tyre was worn out by journey's end.

With our section sold, our ties with Australia were cut. In March 1929, we sailed from Melbourne to Bluff on the *Manuka*, which was to be wrecked on its next voyage. A lot of other things were to be wrecked in the Great Depression, which was soon to strike the world.

[The *Manuka*, a 4534-ton Union Steam Ship Company steamer, was carrying 283 passengers and crew when it struck a reef and sank off the Catlins coast of New Zealand on 16 December 1929. Everyone got off safely into lifeboats, and no lives were lost.]

Chapter 3
BACK IN SOUTHLAND

I had been back in Southland only a few days when I asked some of the motorcycling types what had become of my old Indian. They told me it was in a garage at Riverton. I rode there on the Indian I had brought back from Australia, and found my old bike forlorn in a corner of George McNaught's garage. It had been pulled down and stripped of its parts. George decided it wasn't worth fixing and took it to pieces and put the parts in boxes. He let me have it back for one pound [$2].

While we were in Invercargill, I got in with the Southland Motorcycle Club for the first time. By the time we had left for the bush at Fortification, where I had got a job, I had plans to join in the grass-track racing at Invercargill's Rugby Park. [Fortification is a locality in eastern Southland and the Catlins that grouped sawmilling settlements and forestry in early Southland.] Before that, the man who talked me into joining the club, Harold Jones, a Harley sidecar man, took me on my first trip to the races at Invercargill's Oreti Beach.

Racing was a bit different from a speed trial, but I had my Australian experience. However, Oreti Beach was a little different from the beach racing in Victoria. At Oreti Beach, the boys raced on still-wet sand as the tide went out. Old hands used the oil-based modelling clay Plasticine round their magnetos, and improvised shields to protect their engines from the salt spray. In my first race, I roared to the front, but was drowned out when the water choked my engine. Before the next race, I scouted round the sand hills and found an old kerosene tin. I ripped it in half and wrapped it round the front of the engine to make a rough shield. I roared to the front and stayed there, though the flathead engine overheated. I was first over the finish line, with a trail of smoke behind me.

On the quarter-mile track at Rugby Park, I tried some of the dirt-track tricks I learned in Australia. My broadsiding went down well with the crowd, but wasn't entirely successful for winning races. On grass, you are better to ride the corners. When you get into a spin, you lose your forward speed.

Meanwhile, down in the bush at Fortification, I was getting into my stride as a sawmill's carpenter and millwright. I looked after the mill's tractors and machinery and worked on contract building houses. It was a fairly tough grind. When things were going well, I could knock up a house in four weeks, doing everything myself, from making doors to hanging paper. To do this, I had to work from 5 a.m. to 9 p.m. with one 10-minute break for lunch. For such slavery I earned 35 pounds [$70] per house. Still, I suppose I shouldn't complain. That was a lot more than most of my mates had coming in during the black days of the early 1930s.

At first I spent two days a week on the maintenance work, and later, as orders flowed in to my employer, I worked full-time house building. The mill had wooden tram lines out into the bush to bring in logs. There were about 45 bridges on the lines, and I had to look after these. They hadn't been maintained for two years, and many were nearly rotted away. More than once, the rail tractor I was riding crashed through a bridge.

When I got any spare time I pottered round with the engines of my bikes. After a few months I sold the engine out of my Australian Indian, but kept the frame. Around this time I started getting alloy pistons cast for the flathead engine I had converted to overhead. I made the patterns myself, and had them cast at an Invercargill factory. Then I decided to try casting myself. I started very primitively, using baking-powder tins and dry dirt. Then I began using sand, and eventually got on to die casting. Over the years, I have developed my casting technique, and now think I can tell the temperature of the metal by the look of it. I still use simple methods, though, a blow-lamp and an old cooking pot being my furnace.

I kept up racing, and had a great day at Oreti Beach in 1930. I won three big races — the championship and two long-distance races. That was the year my Indian got dubbed the 'Munro Special'. There used to be grass-track races at country sports meetings in those days. I remember riding at the Waikaia and Riversdale sports meetings. One meeting used to be held on a Saturday, and the other on Easter Monday. There also used to be a mile grass track at the Gore racecourse. I won the last of the competitions on it, held about this time. Southland's famous moonshine, Hokonui, was still being distilled in the hills in those days, and I remember having a glass or two at the meeting. Its action on a human being was a bit like the action of nitro on a racing motorcycle.

As I developed my engine, the conrods began to give me trouble. I must have wrecked 50 in various races. I had to pull out of the 100-mile [161-km] championship at Oreti Beach because of them. A little later they again broke when I was leading in the 12-mile [19.3-km] championship at the Waikouaiti beach races, near Dunedin.

I was coming back to Invercargill that night with Bert Goodwich in his old Essex Tourer. My Indian was tied on one side of the car, and his KTT Velocette was lashed to the other side as we puttered through the night. I was complaining about my conrods. Bert suggested I write to the Indian factory in America and ask Indian to send me out a specially strengthened pair. I thought about this for days afterwards. I didn't think they would make a special pair of conrods for a motorcyclist in the sticks of little New Zealand, and even if they would make them I didn't know what I would pay for them with. There was only one solution: make my own.

Five months later, after spending hours in a blacksmith's shop, I had made a pair by hand out of old Ford truck axles. I used files, hacksaws and a grindstone to get the axles down to the right thickness. Then they weren't quite thick enough, so I heated them until they were white hot and hammered them out a bit.

While I was at the mill, I also built wheels for the bike. Then in early 1932 I had a row with the mill boss and I was out of work. Times were tough, and I took the family to Invercargill and got a job on a relief project at Duck Creek. I worked with hundreds of men from all walks of life who had the choice between this job and starvation. I had a good eye for levels, and many of the men had little experience of manual work, so I was one of the gang put on bringing up the bottom mud in this drainage project. I didn't work at Duck Creek every day. Sometimes I was able to get casual work on the wharves at Bluff, doing carpentry on ships. I lasted three or four months at Duck Creek, then I got a big break. I was offered a job as a travelling salesman for the Invercargill motorcycle firm Tappers.

AT THE END OF 1932, I was riding round Southland selling Triumphs, Velocettes, Francis-Barnetts, BSAs and the occasional

Harley-Davidson. This was work I loved. I was riding and talking motorcycles all day and getting paid for it. I had a lot of spills and laughs and made a lot of sales.

Men would write in from the backblocks inquiring about various bikes, and I would be dispatched to see them, riding one of the half-dozen or so motorcycles I went through every year. I used to modify them and sell them after they had done a thousand or two thousand miles [1610 to 3220 km]. In 10 years working for Tappers, I sold hundreds of bikes. My best run was 44 sales in 42 days. My best sales trip covered 600 miles [965 km], during which I sold nine bikes.

The toughest trip was when I went to the backblocks of Te Anau in 1936. I was riding a new Velocette, the first MAC model to come to Southland. Some fellows at Prospect Flat, on the back of Mararoa sheep station, had written in to Tappers. They gave their address as Mararoa Station, which wasn't too difficult to reach by the standards of the day — or it wouldn't have been if there hadn't been so much frost about at the time. Southland's new Caroline–Josephville road had just opened. I rode over it and found it like riding on an ice rink, there had been so many heavy frosts. I virtually skidded up and over the hills, then I was on my way to Lumsden and Mararoa. I reached the station homestead and was told the men were at Prospect Flat. When I told the people there I would ride over on my bike, they laughed, and said it was impossible. No one had got through with a motor vehicle before.

It wasn't impossible, but it was damned tough going. I began to think that the people at the homestead might have been right when I came across a Ford car abandoned on the track halfway to the flat. Darkness was coming, but I thought it would be just as tough getting back to the homestead as pressing on, so I went on. I was thrown off the bike several times a mile, but I eventually made it through the tussock swamp to the little hut where the men — musterers — were camped.

They were more than a little surprised when I arrived on

the bike, but the performance didn't help to make any sales. While we sat around a roaring wood fire in the little hut as the southern frost set in, I gave my sales patter. Unfortunately, the fellows didn't have enough money.

In the morning, I rode in low gear back through the tussocks to the homestead, back onto the main road, and up to Te Anau. My next stop was the public works camp up the Hollyford Valley. I wanted to see some men at Monkey Flat, by the Homer Tunnel. The only road up the valley was a big ditch, four-feet five-inches [1.4 metres] wide. The workmen had dug this in preparation for the road they were to build.

Small creeks had to be forded. On the deeper ones there were little footbridges for the men to cross. I crossed a few successfully, but as I neared Monkey Flat I was crossing one of the log constructions when I saw a three-foot [0.9-metre] gap ahead of me. I couldn't stop without losing my balance and thus crashing down into the creek. So I gave the bike full throttle, held my breath, and flew across like a Hollywood stuntman.

I couldn't cross the last obstacle, Monkey Creek, so I parked the Velocette and walked to the camp. One of the first men I met was a church missionary out to look after the souls of the workers. He told me the boys at the camp could hear the noise of the bike for about an hour. No motor vehicle had been up the valley till then, not even a tractor, and they had been looking for an aeroplane. I don't remember whether I sold any bikes there, but I enjoyed the trip, though over two days I rode 54 miles [87 km] in low gear.

The Queenstown–Kingston road round the side of Lake Wakatipu hadn't been finished then, and I was sent off to see a prospect at the camp where men building the Staircase bridge were living. To get there, I had to go around the lake's gravel beach. It was very heavy going, and I put the Velocette 500 I was riding in low gear and walked alongside, pushing it, to get through. Another time I rode over rocky hills at Shingle Creek in Central Otago to sell a bike to a trapper who used it to go round his trap lines.

Salesmen know no hours of work. One day selling bikes in Central Otago, I had been working for many hours by the time I reached my last contact, who worked on a farm at Earnscleugh. I got the farmer out of bed, and he directed me to a hut at the back of the house, where the farmhand slept. I woke him, and made a sale at 2 a.m. He signed the papers and gave me some cash and a motorcycle as a trade-in. I rode his bike to Alexandra, got a brief sleep at a hotel, then was up at 5 a.m. to put the machine on the rail. Then I went back out to the farm in a taxi to pick up my machine. I had an appointment to see a client outside the Invercargill post office at 10 a.m., and on the way I had another prospect at Croydon, near Gore. I kept both appointments.

I had one bad spill in my early sales years. I was on a sales trip to the outback Lilburn district in Western Southland. I left Tuatapere on my Harley Colt and was heading up the Waiau Valley to Clifden when I came across a rider on the roadside with an Indian Scout, broken down. We got his bike going and, as he, too, was headed for the lime works, I volunteered to ride behind him and to give him a tow if he broke down again.

Just as we passed the corner of the Lilburn turn-off a dog ran onto the road. I hit him with my front wheel, and down I went in a shower of gravel. When I came to, I was alone. There was no sign of the other rider. I crawled out from under the Harley and went to a nearby farmhouse. The farmer's wife washed the blood from my face, but of course the farm didn't own the dog that had shot out of the farmhouse hedge and brought me down. The spill flattened the tank on the Harley.

Hens from farms always seemed to be running in front of me as I toured around. I always travelled fast. I liked to cruise at 70 miles per hour [112.6 km/h] where possible, and this made it a little hard for them to get out of my road. I was selling in the Arrowtown district and called on a farmer. His wife told me he was working on a water race.

'Take the side road and keep looking up at the water race. You should see him,' she said.

I cut my cruising speed to 60 miles per hour [96.6 km/h] and took off down the little road, with one eye on the water race. I was passing a farmhouse when I looked ahead and saw a hen running flat out across the road. There was a whirr, and I was sure I had collected it. I kept on round a corner and came to the end of the road. I couldn't see the man I was looking for, so I turned to go back down the road. As I came to the farmhouse near where I had skittled the hen I saw three men on the roadside.

'Uh, oh,' I thought. 'How much is a hen worth?'

I pulled up alongside the three: a farmer and his two sons. They all looked about seven foot [2.13 metres] high. I made some polite conversation and cast my eye around for the dead hen. I couldn't see it, though there were plenty of feathers.

'Plenty of bloody feathers around,' grumbled the farmer as he and his sons kicked stones with their boots. Then I saw it — alive, standing forlornly beside the house and utterly bald. There wasn't a feather left on it. I was hard put to stop bursting into laughter as I kick-started the bike, farewelled the farmer and his sons, and roared down the road.

Another time, a black hen ran out in front of me. There was a smack, but I couldn't see it anywhere and kept going. When I stopped a few miles down the road I found it hanging under the bike, by the neck.

THROUGHOUT THE 1930s, I MODIFIED the Indian and raced on the beach and competed in hill climbs and time trials. I even tried to have a go on the 'wall of death' at a sideshow when the Royal Agricultural Show was held in Invercargill. The sideshow owner wouldn't let me. He reckoned I was too old. I tried to sneak up the wall when he was outside, but he heard me revving the bike and banned me before I had enough speed to start climbing.

Some of the local riders rode the wall. One of them, Owen Wale, blacked out when he was up the wall. He got down somehow and fell off the bike, which then roared round by itself, out of control. I was inside the wall at the time, and darted and dodged as the bike zoomed around and crashed off the wall. I managed to grab it and cut the motor, but not before it crashed across my leg, crushing my foot. That episode, which put me off work for a week, cured my desire to ride the 'wall of death'.

[The wall of death, a sideshow developed in America in 1915, continues today in countries including Britain and India. It is a large wooden cylinder, 20 feet to 36 feet (6.1 to 11 metres) in diameter, in which motorcyclists travel around and up the vertical wall, helped by centripetal force. The audience stands around the top of the cylinder and looks down on the motorcyclists. At the Invercargill A&P (Agricultural & Pastoral) show — what in some countries would be called a country fair — the wall of death was a great attraction for youngsters, most of whose parents were warning them they had better not think of getting a motorbike when they were older. The 'wall' comprised a cylinder of vertical boards. The roar of the engine was magnified, fumes poured out the top, and the whole board cylinder shook as a bike whirred around, rising higher to the painted limit near the top. A treat was when two bikes were both roaring round the wall.]

The beach races were the highlight of the year for me. I used to live for them. There were about three race meetings every summer at Oreti Beach, and they had a big public following. Up to 13,000 people would turn out to watch. We would work all year on our bikes to prepare for these. It was comparatively safe racing, and far safer than riding than on the Teretonga track. You could follow every man's position all the way. I have seen

25 riders start off scratch on a championship race at the beach.

You would know the date and live for the racing for weeks beforehand, then an hour before they were due to start there would be a storm and they would be put off. That was heartbreaking. Two or three days after a wind storm and after a right tide, the sand would be hard and smooth like a billiard table. Too much fine weather made the beach soft and unusable.

On the beach I could get a decent run and try out the Indian. Over the years, I have improved her by about three miles an hour per year. More often than not I blew out some part of the engine. By doing this you learn the weak parts that need to be modified and can go even faster before the engine packs up again.

In 1937, I had my only bad crash in beach racing while riding in a 20-mile [32.2-km] event on Oreti Beach. I was on the back mark, but by the second-last lap I had caught everyone in the field except Ewart Currie. I was doing about 110 miles per hour [177 km/h] and Ewart was about 50 yards [45.7 metres] in front of me. The sand was even inside my goggles, and I couldn't see the pylon that marked the end of the straight.

'I'll just follow Ewart round,' I thought to myself. It didn't register that the wet sand might obstruct his vision, too.

Next thing, Ewart swung in front of me, slowing. I slammed straight into him, square on. I could see he was going to turn, and I was just about to cut my engine and slam on the little original six-inch [15.2-cm] brake on the Indian when I hit him.

Ewart went down, and I went sailing through the air in one direction while the Indian went in another. I crashed heavily on the wet sand, and Ewart's machine, bouncing along the beach, came down on top of me. My crash hat took most of the impact of the bike. The hat split and I went out like a light. The attendants sprinted up the beach to pick up Ewart and me.

My brother joked afterwards he spent an age picking up gold-filled teeth scattered on the sand. I came down about 15 feet [4.6 metres] from the impact stop, my brother told me.

The Indian went up the beach for 120 feet [36.6 metres]. I was knocked out, but not too badly hurt. I don't think Ewart was permanently damaged, either.

ABOUT 1936, I STARTED GOING to Christchurch every year to see the New Zealand motorcycle Grand Prix. There was a lot of interest in it in those days, and thousands of spectators thronged the 6.2-mile [10-km] circuit. It was gravel, and I can remember not being over-impressed by the performance on the loose surface by some of the riders.

I made the mistake of remarking to mates who went with me to the races one year that if I couldn't ride better on the gravel than some of those jokers, I would go home. They held me to it, and talked me into entering the next year.

That was 1938. I needed big brakes and a foot gear-change for the Grand Prix, so I couldn't use the Indian. I got hold of a 1937 Velocette. The rules of the race said you weren't allowed to alter the bike, but I inserted some home-made parts. I made cams for it, rebuilt the racing carburettor, changed some of the alterable parts such as handlebars and seat position, and put alloy mudguards on it.

First I had to get from Invercargill to Christchurch. I left at 12.10 p.m. and I was in Christchurch at 6.30 p.m. for tea. I think that would be a pretty good time nowadays, with bitumen road all the way. In those days the road was a little longer, and on it I had to contend with 100 miles [161 km] of gravel.

I went up on the Saturday and missed the pre-race practice. When I ran across the road and onto my bike in the Le Mans start on Monday I still didn't know the circuit. The flag came down, we raced to our bikes, and roared off. The pay-off for not knowing the course came at the end of the back straight, first time round. It was on me before I knew it was there, and suddenly I was flying through gorse bushes and long grass. I hung on like grim death and got through and back onto the track without coming off.

For the first 17 laps of the race, every lap my time got lower and I got the feel for the course. By the 100-mile [161-km] mark, I was in the lead, three minutes ahead of the rest of the field. I pulled in for fuel. Just as I was pushing to get started again, two bikes ripped past me in a shower of gravel, and the motor, which had just then started, was cut dead. A stone had been sucked under the inlet valve. Desperate, I cut a piece out of the valve. As a little fuel seeped in, the bike began to fire a bit. I picked up a bit of speed for a while, but I got slower and slower, though I had the throttle wide open. Despite this, I managed to finish second to Bobby Stewart, who was on a Rudge Ulster.

About 1938, I was on my way to work at Tappers. A Ford car was slowing up as I overtook it. Just as it stopped, a dog jumped out from in front of it and rushed straight into my front wheel. I went clean over the handlebars and was concussed for a short time. I got up, cussed the dog, and rode the bike to Tappers. I walked round for a while, and woke up three hours later in hospital. I gradually recovered.

In 1939, I was back for another crack at the Grand Prix, with the same bike going faster, but the top came clean off a piston, and I coasted into the pit without using the brakes. I rode in the event again in 1940 and mechanical failure beat me for the third time in a row.

THE INDIAN HADN'T BEEN FORGOTTEN, and I slaved away at it in my spare time. Dies made from axles I found in a city street helped me to keep a good supply of pistons. I fitted a two-row primary chain and installed Indian Prince forks. Extensive drilling to such parts as the rocker supports and brake anchors, and the use of alloy wherever possible, helped me keep down the weight of the machine.

In 1940, the machine was ready for big things. On January 27, I had the bike at Main West Road, Aylesbury, outside Christchurch [perhaps what is now called the Old West Coast Road]. Over the flying half-mile [805 metres], I clocked one run of 130 miles per hour [209.2 km/h] and another of 110 miles per hour [177 km/h], giving me an average of 120.8 miles per hour [194.4 km/h], a New Zealand speed record which was to stand for 12 years.

The old 1920 Indian, serial number 50R627, guaranteed by the maker to do 'more than 50 miles per hour [80.5 km/h]' had come a long way. With my modifications over nearly 20 years, the engine capacity increased from 596 cc to 608 cc and many new parts were substituted. Basically, however, the Special was the same dogged Indian Scout.

One of my innovations in 1940 was my first effort at streamlining. My streamliner that year was merely a tiny hood with two peepholes, but its success set me on a long path which eventually led to full streamline shells.

[Burt made four streamliners. He hammered the first one out of aluminium. He built the second in fibreglass, but with a triple tail fin of aluminium. The third streamliner, which he used from 1963 to 1966, also of fibreglass, had a single tail fin. The fourth streamliner, in fibreglass, had a longer tail fin and a slightly different nose. Burt used this from 1969 to 1971.]

In 1940, I set a record for the Bluff Hill climb, a big event on the local motorcycling calendar. Then the black clouds of World War II gradually fogged out the sport for a few years.

THE WAR MADE THINGS TOUGH for a travelling salesman. Petrol was rationed. At first, I was limited to about 80 gallons [302.8 litres] a month, which was just enough to enable me to keep on my work. When the Japanese hit Pearl Harbor, my ration was chopped to six gallons [22.7 litres] a month. That would have ended my selling career if I hadn't been thinking of something that was going to get me out of just such a jam.

This was a gas producer. Quite a number of cars had these fitted during the war. They were really blast furnaces. The engine started on petrol, then switched on to gas from the furnace, which ran on coal from which tar had been removed.

When I finished my gas producer, it was, as far as I know, the first in the world for a motorcycle. I fitted it on to my 500 cc Speed Twin Triumph. It was a great success. I would start on petrol then switch over. The set-up was best when I opened the throttle full out and shut the petrol completely off. This meant my cruising speed was constant. It couldn't be varied unless I leaned down and turned off the gas, but it produced excellent results in saving petrol. The best performance I got was 600 miles [965.6 km] using only one quart [1.14 litres] of petrol.

[George Begg says in his book *Burt Munro: Indian Legend of Speed* that Burt's gas producer was in a container beside the rear wheel. On the other side of the wheel was a cyclone gas filterer and the fuel — coal partly burned to reduce tar. This burned slowly, giving off gas, which replaced the usual petrol. Performance was about two-thirds of that with petrol.]

I had been thinking about a gas producer for a while, but the thing that finally started me building was when I came home from Central Otago on the night of the Pearl Harbor attack. The service station man told me there was to be no more fuel sold after six o'clock that night. I bought a five-gallon drum off him with my [wartime rationing] coupons and rode home with it propped on the tank.

Within two weeks my gas producer was fitted and working. It was a great asset to a salesman. While everyone else was semi-grounded because of the fuel shortage, I was able to get about to my clients. In one six-week period I travelled 1000 miles [1609 km] a week with the aid of the burner. But in the long run it was to be the cause of my giving up salesmanship, and even nearly the death of me. It happened about 14 months after I began using the producer.

We were buying up used motorcycles because no new ones were being imported. I left early one morning up the Invercargill–Queenstown highway to buy a Velocette. I was cruising at 55 to 60 miles per hour [88.5 to 96.6 km/h] along the gravel road at Ryal Bush with the gas on and the petrol off.

Suddenly I saw a patch of gravel ahead of me that was so thick I knew I would go over in it. I held onto the handlebars tight and, as we hit the gravel, managed to get a little control for a while, but then the bike slewed out of control onto the grass on the roadside. I regained control before the bike ripped into the wire fenceline back from the road, then we were roaring uphill along the grass verge. I hadn't been able to let the handlebars go for an instant to cut off the gas.

It was like riding a mad beast. I still had hopes of getting one hand down to the gas control when a huge gap opened in front of me. It was a cutting in the hillside for a farmer's road off the main route. I hung on as the machine and I became airborne for a fraction of a second, then we ricocheted off the other side of the cutting and soared through the air. When I came round an hour later I couldn't see for blood in my eyes.

I was lying on the gravel with my hands still on the handlebars of the bike, which lay sprawled in the gravel behind me. Wiping the blood from my eyes, I staggered to my feet and surveyed the damage. The back wheel had apparently absorbed the shock of our landing. The wheel rim was bashed right up to the hub.

The woman in the farmhouse washed my wounds and

phoned my employers, who came out and picked me up. I was a mess. For a week my nose bled, and a medical specialist in Dunedin told me I had a haemorrhage in the front of my brain. My skull wasn't broken, but the medical man told me it would have been better if it had cracked and absorbed more of the impact. I wished I had been wearing a hard crash hat. In those days on the roads we wore leather helmets.

After 11 months off work recovering from the injuries, and with a strict warning from the specialist not to get on a motorcycle for at least four years, I gave up my sales job. I didn't recover fully for a long time. I suffered from intense headaches for nearly 20 years. However, long before they stopped, I took a new job when I felt well enough. This was as a travelling buyer.

I WORKED FOR A TIMARU firm which bought used American cars in good condition and shipped them back to the United States, where the market was better than in New Zealand. Times certainly have changed. We pay more than twice the price of new American cars for vehicles that, in America, would long ago have been compressed into a bale of metal in a junk yard.

This job kept me in bread for the next two or three years. The only motorcycling I did was to take the family out to Riverton Rocks beach occasionally in a little trailer I made to tow behind the Indian Scout. I had four children — far too many for the sidecar. Johnny, the youngest, was aged about four. [Johnny's elder siblings were Gwen, June and Margaret.]

When I first used the little two-wheel trailer back in the 1930s, I hooked it to a 500 Velocette with a coupling bolted direct to the back of the carrier. I got only a few hundred yards when it threw all the kids out onto the road, put me into a speed wobble, and tipped me off. We eventually got to the Rocks. The kids were bruised a bit, and my wife — well, she had been on the back behind me. At the picnic, I soon had to take all young hands for rides in the trailer. As soon as we got moving at any speed the trailer would take off. So I took the family home.

After this, I made a different drawbar. Instead of coupling it to the carrier, it had a heel on it, and was connected to the back axle. With this, I could tow the trailer at 70 miles per hour [112.7 km/h] in perfect safety. Later, after I had no need for it, I learned such a coupling was illegal. Finally, I converted the trailer into a little cart on which my father could sit behind his horse-drawn harrows while cultivating.

In 1945, I suffered another accident, this time not connected with motorcycling. My wife was making soap and I bumped into her as she was walking past into the laundry with a basin of boiling caustic soda. The soda spilled over me and knocked me clean out. A neighbour rushed me to hospital, and they put me in a saline bath. For 11 days I teetered between life and death before I started to pick up. I was in hospital for weeks and weeks, then on VJ night ['Victory over Japan' — celebrations marking the end of World War II], I was released from hospital.

Bandaged up and aching, I reached the home I had built in Tramway Road, South Invercargill 14 years before. No one was home. I went to my father's nearby farm, Elston Lea, and stayed the night. I had some pain, and couldn't sleep. Something kept urging me, 'Go to the house! Go to the house!' until I drifted to sleep about 3 a.m. At 4 a.m., my brother came upstairs and woke me. He had been at a dance.

'Have you insured your house?' he asked me.

My home was on fire.

I had only 500 pounds [$1000] of insurance to cover everything. My brother told me I couldn't do anything. The house, only half a mile [800 metres] away, was already in the grip of flames. From my bed I could hear jars of preserved fruit exploding as the house burned down. My trophies, my photographs, my clippings from 26 years of motorcycling, were lost.

A few months later my wife and I parted ways for ever, and a new era in my life was about to open. At an age when most men are settling into the carpet-slippers stage, I was flung into a new chapter of my life. [Burt was 46.]

For two years from 1945, I was a businessman, or tried to be a businessman. With Mac Tulloch, I took over a fleet of 12 trucks at Mataura and became a carrier. It was tough slogging. I worked 100 hours a week maintaining the trucks and driving. I spent Sundays building a house, so there was no time for motorcycling. I was so tied up with work in those two years that I got down to Invercargill only once.

By 1947, I had had enough. I decided I would rather be a poor man than a rich machine. So I sold my share of the business to Mac [the Tulloch family stayed in the carrying firm, building it into a large regional business], and I bought half my father's farm at Elston Lea. Dad had been trying to retire, and had sold the other half. And I got back to motorcycling.

Chapter 4
TO AUSTRALIA AGAIN

The old Indian was soon in pieces again as I returned to tinkering. There were hill climbs and speed trials and beach racing. Before I knew where I was, it was 1948. For some reason I began to feel old, and got a yearning to go to Australia and look up old friends before they or I died. I called at a shipping office in Invercargill one afternoon and they told me a freighter was sailing for China from Bluff that very day, and if I had called earlier I could have sailed on her. What time did she sail?

'You would have to be at Bluff at 4 p.m. with your luggage,' said the clerk.

It was about 3 p.m. I rushed across to the bank to get the 21-pound [$42] fare and arrange for drafts to be sent to me monthly. The bank's main door was closed, but the manager was a friend and let me in through the side door. I picked up a clearance from the Tax Department, picked up a pair of socks, a shirt, underwear and a suitcase, and raced the 16 miles [25.8 km] to Bluff. I made it by 4 p.m.

[The tax clearance was likely to have been a requirement of the ship's captain in an over-zealous interpretation of the tax regulations of the day, which in some cases empowered Customs to stop a ship from sailing over unpaid tax.]

I returned to Invercargill and said goodbye to my daughter and her husband, who were living in a new house I had built at the Tramway Road site, and at midnight I sailed for Australia. The night we sailed, Australia devalued its currency, which put me into even more of a holiday mood. Four other men from Southland were passengers on the ship and I chummed up with one, Mac, from Te Anau. After we landed in Sydney, he and I stayed only a day or two before we flew to Brisbane.

My friend was keen to see dirt-track racing and we reached the track about 6.30 p.m. With us were two girls we met at a little shop that sold lottery tickets. We were about to go into the track when Mac said he wanted some beer. The girls said they wouldn't go in with us if we took beer. Mac persisted, the girls disappeared, then Mac found you couldn't buy beer in the suburbs after about 6 p.m., though you could in the centre of Brisbane. Mac decided to go there and look for beer, and asked where I would be sitting. By the time Mac got back, there were about 25,000 people at the track and he didn't have a hope of finding me.

A scratch race was being run on the heavy yellow shale track later in the programme, when a rider on one of the latest five-stud J.A.P.s hit a small patch that was still wet from a shower during the day. He went into a slide and came out with his back wheel spinning so fast it ripped a chunk out of the track and sent it flying into the spectators. Out of the 25,000 people there, the fist-sized chunk hit me. It knocked me off my seat into the laps of the people sitting behind me. I was blinded. It raced through my mind that my eye was hurt, and I remembered a Central Otago trapper I had sold a bike to. A piece of wire ripped his eye. The first he knew of it was when the white of his eye dripped down onto his boots.

I held my handkerchief over my eye and staggered across the track to where I had seen some ambulance men on the opposite side. I knew from the quietness that the race had finished. The ambulance men bandaged my eyes with wadding, and my Te Anau mate raced across after seeing me stagger across the track.

The ambulance men took me and Mac to the Brisbane general hospital nearby and I was put in the eye ward. While we were waiting, we struck up acquaintance with a young man in the ward from Kingaroy [210 km from Brisbane, Australia's peanut-growing capital and home town of former Queensland Premier Sir Joh Bjelke-Petersen]. We could hear the bikes racing on the speedway.

A doctor came round and looked at my eye. He said it was so bad it would have to come out. Mac, my new friend from Kingaroy, and I let out howls of protest that included threats of violence. The doctor said he would wait till morning and let a specialist look at it.

The specialist arrived at 8 a.m. and said he thought he could save the eye. Mac, who had waited through the night, seemed as relieved as I did. It was five days before I could see out of either eye, and I was sweating. On the fifth day I saw big, pink-looking clouds rolling over the sky. I was even more relieved when the specialist said again he thought he could save the eye.

Three weeks later, when I was discharged, Mac was nearly broke. I took him out to a sawmill and talked the boss into giving him a job. I felt I needed compensation for the eye injury, so I went to the manager of the speedway, Frank Arthur, who I had seen performing as a speedway star in the 1920s. Frank told me people went to the speedway at their own risk, as all the signs over the entrances pointed out. Only once had the speedway paid compensation, when a bike landed in a woman's lap. However, he was prepared to meet me part of the way. Between him and his insurance company my hospital expenses were met and I was given 10 pounds [$20] compensation.

I continued my Australian holiday alone while Mac restored his pocketbook at the sawmill. I spent a few days in Sydney, went down to Mildura to see an old motorcycling friend, then rode on a bus to Adelaide. There I had the last adventure of the trip.

It was a month or so after the eye accident and I was sitting in a restaurant awaiting my order. A soldier sat down beside me, bet me the bent knife I had been given would break, and when it didn't break he threatened me. I was looking at him with my dark glasses off when he hit me with a haymaker, blackening my good eye. I got him in a wrestling hold. Next thing, tables and diners were spinning in all directions as in a Wild West movie.

The manager parted us, allowed us to finish our meals at separate tables, and the soldier challenged me to meet him in the restaurant next day. He didn't show up. I still had the black eye when I arrived home in Invercargill a week later.

Chapter 5
MY LIFE'S PATH: THE INDIAN

B ack in New Zealand, I made a big decision. I would spend the rest of my life working on the Indian. Instead of motorcycling being a hobby, I would make it the main object of my life. Outside work would be for finance.

With the end of the war, the sport of motorcycling boomed in New Zealand. It was the sport's heyday. It gave me plenty of encouragement for the work on the Indian. I had already switched the bike over to foot gear-change. I modified the frame a dozen times. I experimented with short and long pipes, and with windscreens. As usual, while I was working hard on the machine, I had lots of breakdowns and blow-ups. I would adapt one part, she would go a few miles per hour faster, and another part would collapse under stress.

I raced at Oreti Beach and won the occasional race, but as

often as not the bike packed up near the beer parlour. This was the sidecar marking the end of the course. It was up the beach from the spectators. Sam Fraser, a motorcycle mechanic at my old employers, Tappers, was the timekeeper. His 1924 Indian and sidecar held beer purchased by racers for just such eventualities as breakdowns. Sam's offsider was usually Graham Lindsay. The sidecar had a rude nickname that meant girl catcher, but I doubt it had a girl in it in its life.

The beer was made by an old Invercargill brewery, Whitty's, which has long since closed down. The boys used to joke that it had such a kick you could race on it. I thought it was made from Waihopai River water, and anyone who has been to Invercargill should know how strong it was from that. I don't know if it was the beer, but sometimes we got caught out a little by incoming tides. I remember racing in one event towards the end of an afternoon. In the last lap, I got caught by a wave and the engine was drowned. After the races we would all adjourn to a crib [holiday house] for a party into the small hours of the next morning.

[IN 1949, BURT'S FATHER DIED. Burt had earlier bought part of his farm.]

The first year I had the little farm, I bought a horse-drawn mower, cut the grass, made hay, and sold it for cash. Then I leased the grazing rights to a farmer for 150 pounds [$300] so I could devote my time to the Indian. The following year I tried farming for myself.

As a youth, I had been involved only with dairy farming. Now I decided to learn about sheep. Until then, all I knew was that you could shear wool from their backs. I bought 300 ewes, put them to the ram, lambed them, then sold the lambs and shore the ewes. It was the first year of the wool boom. I made

2000 pounds [$4000 — prices soared with the Korean War, and reached an astonishing price for the time of one pound currency for one pound weight].

———————————————— 35 ————————————————

IN 1951, AT THE TIMARU speed trials, Les Lamb, from Oamaru, riding a 1000 cc Vincent HRD, broke my 1940 record for the flying half-mile [0.8 km] with two runs of 142.6 miles per hour [229.5 km/h] and 136.36 miles per hour [219.5 km/h]. I also bettered my old record by more than 10 miles per hour [16.1 km/h], with an average speed of 133.3 miles per hour [214.5 km/h] on two runs — the second fastest time of the day, and the fastest for an unstreamlined machine.

When I had the Munro Special up to this peak, I began monkeying around with another old Indian I found rusting in a South Invercargill hedge years before and bought for five pounds [$10]. It had a 1916 Indian Powerplus frame. I built an overhead valve for it and modified a carburettor to fit it. Then I thought I would attempt to build a double overhead camshaft for it. I built the overhead camshaft and drove it with a chain drive from the time case to the cam box. While I was working on it, I had great difficulty opening the valves, even with a shifting wrench. The answer was rounded valve caps, which I got to work, though there was one drawback: they had to be hand-oiled every time I used her.

The first day I had the remodelled engine in the frame, I took the bike outside and started her. The engine burst into the most wonderful crackle I have ever heard on a motorcycle. Some fellow fans who lived a mile [1.6 km] away at Georgetown heard the noise and ran across the paddocks of the little farm to see what the machine was. We christened the machine the 'double-knocker'.

I built a 900-yard [823-metre] track around one of the paddocks for it, and I encased its chain drive. It was fantastic to ride. It could rev so fast that no one could hold it. The revs would rise to 10,000 per minute without valve float. The double-knocker had standard 1925 Indian Prince flywheels. These increased the stroke to three and a half inches [8.89 cm] from thirty-one sixteenths [4.72 cm], which is standard for a Scout. By making my own cylinders, I brought the capacity up to 348 cc. It was great to race on. I was never fully extended.

I rode it only once on what was to become the centre of grass-track riding in Southland after World War II, the Invercargill Showgrounds, and I had one of the most hilarious rides of a lifetime. Coming into the straight at the end of the fourth lap, the motor cut. I looked down — and there was no fuel tank there! I slowed halfway down the straight and turned round to look for the tank. I was so engrossed I was nearly cut down by three J.A.P.s that were chasing me from the scratch mark. I found out later that I had done a whole lap without a tank.

Chapter 6
BRITAIN AND EUROPE, 1955

In April 1955, I sailed to Britain in the liner *Rangitane*, and returned to Invercargill in October. I saw the Isle of Man TT and all the big Continental races. I saw the Moto Guzzi eight-cylinder road racer, the most fabulous motorbike ever built. I watched it run in practice for the Belgian Grand Prix, and I slept above it in a hotel near Spa, Belgium. It was in the basement. I was on the first floor. I asked Ken Kavanagh, the Australian champion who was riding it, if I could look at the machine.

'Burt, if you were my own brother, I would not be allowed to let you look at it.'

He used to pick me up every morning and take me to the track. The Moto Guzzi blew up in one run. The big end packed up, and they took it back to Italy.

[Ken Kavanagh won the 1952 350 cc Ulster Grand Prix, and the 1956 Junior TT at the Isle of Man TT. The Moto Guzzi V8 was capable of 172 mph, or 280 km/h. It was decades ahead of its time but encountered many mechanical problems. The water-cooled engine had 90-degree V cylinders set transversely across the frame.]

I saw the German TT, the Dutch TT, the Belgian Grand Prix, French national scrambles, the Isle of Man, and racing at Crystal Palace and Brands Hatch, London. I saw the first Thruxton 500-mile [805-km] race, near the Salisbury Plain. [The Thruxton 500 was a nine-hour endurance event on an old war airfield near Andover.]

At a big dance at the Empress Hotel, on the Isle of Man, I met greats of motorcycle racing. It was one of the greatest occasions I ever attended. I rode round the Isle of Man. I met Geoff Duke, one of the greatest motorcycle racers of all time, Stanley Woods, and Harold Daniell. At the dance, a young woman sitting near me caught my eye and I danced with her for much of the evening. A public relations man who seemed to know everyone late in the evening asked if I would like to meet Duke. He brought him across, and he was the young woman's husband.

[Duke, an Englishman, won six world championships and six Isle of Man TT races, and was the world's most famous motorcycle racer. Woods, an Irishman who began racing in 1921 on a Harley-Davidson, had 29 Grand Prix wins and won the Isle of Man TT 10 times. Englishman Harold Daniell held an Isle of Man TT lap record for 12 years. The New Zealand team at the Isle of Man that year comprised Bill Collett, Fred Cook, and John Hempleman. Hempleman captained the New Zealand team at the Isle of Man two years later and went on to a distinguished international career as a race rider. He won 10 international grand prix events and was sixth in the world

350 cc championships in 1958, and sixth in the 125 cc world championships in 1960.]

[FROM THE ISLE OF MAN, Burt went to Europe for the motorcycle racing circuit and was at the 1955 Dutch TT at Assen, in north Holland. The three New Zealand team members competed in the Belgian Grand Prix, where Fred Cook remembers meeting Burt Munro, and Bill Collett was injured in a spill and returned to Britain. That year at Assen, independent (non-works) race riders, known as privateers, had a dispute with organisers that led to Duke, who rode for Gilera, and 14 privateer riders, including Hempleman, being suspended from international competition for six months. Three Italian riders were suspended for four months. The draconian suspension, which attracted widespread criticism from sports fans, meant Hempleman couldn't compete in the Isle of Man in 1956. In 1957, he was back there as captain of the New Zealand team. The suspension was particularly hard on Duke, who seemed to have regarded himself as being a mediator trying to settle the dispute. He never won a major title race after Assen.

Burt's account of this famous motorcycle racing incident was a little foggy, but I was able to talk to John Hempleman and Fred Cook in 2015. The Dutch TT was one of the biggest on the European racing calendar, drawing up to 200,000 spectators, and the privateer riders felt the start money they received of about 20 pounds ($40) was too little. They pulled out of the 350 cc TT, leaving the Moto Guzzi works riders circulating by themselves. The privateers then asked Duke for support for a similar boycott in the 500 cc event. The privateers had backed Duke two years earlier at a similar dispute in the Italian Grand Prix at Monza. Duke agreed to approach the Assen organising officials, who eventually agreed to lift the start money. Duke rode and won the 500 cc event, but says he didn't realise the privateers had held out for higher start money for the 350 cc race as well as the 500 cc event. Duke said he hadn't been aware of this at the time. Fred Cook says:

At the 1955 Dutch TT, John Hempleman and myself were able to take over the start of an English rider who was unable to attend. The Dutch organisers, KNMV, wanted written authorisation from the original entrant, Charlie Fougere. This we were able to get by letter, and all was settled. John would ride his 350 Norton in the 350 race, and I would ride my Matchless G45 in the 500 race. We were camped in the riders' camp, and next day were visited by Australian and English privateer riders, which we were ourselves. They said they were not satisfied with the poor start money being offered. They said they had approached the organisers to have it increased, but were met with instant refusal. Their next move was to organise a strike in the 350 race. The idea was that all privateer riders would pull out of the race after one lap. They wanted John and me to be part of their strike. At first we refused because we felt we were fortunate even to have starts at the meeting. They came back twice more pestering us to join, and it began to look like, if they were successful in their bid for more money, we would be regarded as the 'black sheep' of the privateers. Reluctantly, we joined. The rumour was that organisers got wind of the impending strike, but thought the riders were bluffing.

The 350 race started and, as a spectator, I witnessed all the 12 private entrants pull into the pits after one lap — something I had never seen before. This left the remaining factory machines to complete the race, which could be described as a complete fiasco. As the starting time for the senior TT 500 race drew near, riders' representatives and the organisers met. This time the riders had as their spokesmen the Gilera works team's Geoff Duke and Reg Armstrong [the Irish rider who, later, in the early 1960s, managed the Honda team that won five world titles over 1962 and 1963]. With high-profile riders such as Geoff and Reg acting for them, the privateers seemed to have the clout to reach a satisfactory deal on start money. Geoff Duke and Reg Armstrong had nothing to gain from the row, and I think it was very good of them to help. I can't remember the exact increase, but I think the start money was doubled.

The 500 senior TT race went ahead with no further trouble, and Duke won on a Gilera. This was on 20 June 1955 and the Commission Sportive Internationale the CSI of the Fédération Internationale de Motocyclisme, the FIM, or world motorcycle racing federation, meeting on 24 September, imposed a six-month suspension from 1 January to 30 June 1956. This covered the 12 riders who pulled out of the 350 race and Duke and Armstrong. This ruled them out of the Isle of Man TT and several other important races. Whether the 1955 Dutch TT strike was a good idea will always be debatable.]

[JOHN HEMPLEMAN DOESN'T REMEMBER MEETING Burt Munro at the Isle of Man or in Europe. Fred Cook, who does remember Burt at the Belgian Grand Prix, recalls someone at one stage asking Burt where he slept the night before. Burt said, 'Under a truck.' Because he rode in the 500 race after the Assen organisers compromised, Fred was not suspended. Over 1955 and 1956, he won four silver replicas on the Isle of Man, two each in the senior TT and junior TT. Silver replicas are awarded to riders who complete the course within eleven tenths (110 per cent) of the winner's time.

The use of 'TT', from 'Tourist Trophy', has been adopted for motorcycle races in many parts of the world, but in Europe when Burt was there, apart from the Isle of Man and Dutch TTs, countries called their main motorcycle race a grand prix. The original Isle of Man event more than a century ago was called 'tourist trophy' because it was for 'touring' motorcycles. Sometimes 'TT' is wrongly interpreted as 'time trial'. Not so — it is for races.]

IT WAS THE BEST BRITISH summer for years, and when I left I wanted to come back through the United States, but I couldn't get suitable ships. I couldn't even get a passage on a traditional route until someone cancelled. I sat on a doorstep till I got a cancellation. It took me as far as Brisbane in a beautiful ship, the *Strathnaver*. There I changed ships and came home.

When I was in Germany I heard that NSU was going to the Bonneville Salt Flats the next year for a world record attempt, and I was determined to be there. Meanwhile, at home in Invercargill, I worked full-time on the Indian.

Chapter 7
FIRST US TRIP, 1956: YEAR OF THE CHEVROLET

[The interview notes are light on details of Burt's trip to Britain, Europe, and especially the Isle of Man in 1955. They return to normal during Burt's description of the first of what would eventually be 14 trips to the United States in 1956. The first American visit was without his Indian. The notes begin with his arrival in Hawaii by ship. He had heard NSU was about to try to break new records at the Bonneville Salt Flats in the United States. NSU Motorenwerke AG, of West Germany, at the time was the world's biggest motorcycle manufacturer. Volkswagen took it over in 1969, and merged it with Auto Union into what became Audi. Burt was accompanying Southlander Russell Wright and his mechanic, Scotsman Bob Burns, on their way to Bonneville, where they hoped to regain the world sidecar record from another German motorcycle maker, BMW. When the liner the three men were travelling on reached Honolulu they learned NSU was planning attempts on solo records.]

I heard in Honolulu that the Germans were starting tests the next day, and we were still 10 days' sailing time to get to the States. I got a reservation on a plane, valid till 4 p.m. I had to get a visa to land in Hawaii before I could get on the plane. I got it, and at three minutes to four I got the last seat on a DC-6B going to San Francisco that night. There was cloud all the way. There was fog over San Francisco. My first glimpse of America was just north of San Francisco — the top of a hill with a highway on it. It was morning, and we had gained three hours.

The next thing was to get into downtown and get a bus to the Salt Lake, 650 miles [1046 km] away. By 4 p.m. I was on a bus, and that night I travelled by Continental Trailways, hitting 72 miles per hour [115.9 km/h].

[To the question, 'How so precise?', Burt replied that he had timed the bus with a stopwatch.]

My first glimpse of the Salt was of it miles away, through a break in the mountains. I saw several square miles of it, and boy did I get a thrill. We arrived at Wendover, near the Salt, next day.

I booked into a motel, put my case in a room, and hitch-hiked to the Salt. Before I knew where I was, a guy in a utility [pick-up truck], who was doing 80 miles per hour [128.8 km/h], gave me a lift. It was only five miles [8 km] away, and I asked, 'Do you have to hurry that much?' The driver said he wasn't used to 'nervous people', but slowed a little before he dropped me off at the Bonneville chain-fence gate.

The first guy I met was Captain Eyston, of world-record-breaking fame. Eyston was there waiting for the Germans to finish. He told me it was 10 miles to where the motorcycles were running. I said, 'I've come a long way.'

[Englishman Captain George Eyston set three land-speed records between 1937 and 1939 in his car *Thunderbolt*.]

I took everything off except my trousers — shoes, socks and shirt — and started walking. I had got about five miles [8 km], when suddenly a Ford Mercury roared up. You could see it was going real fast. It screeched to a halt. The security folk inside asked me what I was doing. I said I had come thousands of miles to see NSU attack the world speed record.

'You have?'

'Sure.'

'Then hop in.'

They took me and introduced me all round to the NSU team of about 40 — to mechanics, press men, ambulance men. They took me under their wing because I had come so far. For 10 days I became part of the team. They gave me jobs. One was judging the wind, sometimes I was just helping around, and some days I was on the spy glass to see nobody came in like I did. On the way back from the course they did 90 miles per hour [144.8 km/h].

I suggested they [the NSU team] should add a mile and a half [2.4 km] for a practice run, and they immediately took it in as part of the run-in. At the end of 10 days, the NSU team had broken 32 records, from 50 cc to the world maximum for a motorcycle. All the machines were streamliners.

After the 10 days, they gave me a souvenir book, and at a bit of a shindig a piece of a cake baked by their main rider, Wilhelm Herz. At one time he had something wrong with his hands, and the doctors told him to learn baking to help. He got to like baking. He made the cake for the celebrations after he set the absolute speed record. Herz's absolute record of 211.54 miles per hour [340.4 km/h] made him the first person to ride a motorcycle over 200 miles per hour [321.9 km/h].

[GETTING A PLACE TO STAY wasn't easy at Wendover, which borders the Bonneville Salt Flats. Wendover is near Utah's border with Nevada, and is 121 miles (194.7 km) west of Salt Lake City.]

I had been in Wendover 10 days with the NSU guys, and was standing outside the Western Motel's café. Two men arrived. One had a Vincent across his T-shirt. I thought I recognised Marty Dickerson, a well-known American Vincent rider. He got an American record of 164 miles per hour [263.9 km/h] for a 1000 cc supercharged machine in 1965. The other guy was Elby Stuart.

[In the 1950s Marty Dickerson set a class record at Bonneville that held for 20 years.]

As soon as they went in, I went over to Elby Stuart and to a young woman, Jackie Robarge, who was to become Mrs Dickerson, and they confirmed the person they were with was indeed Marty Dickerson. They came back from the motel desk and said there wasn't a room left to be had. I invited them to share my room. They spent about four days camped in my room, which I was paying about US$4.50 a day for. They had camper beds with them, and then invited me to go out into the desert with them and share their desert camp. I went. Ever since, they have helped me with my Bonneville speed runs.

The day after the runs ended, they invited me to go to Los Angeles with them in their utility. It was a long 800-mile [1287.5-km] trip [Burt was on the tray at the back]. When we got there I bought a Chevrolet, one-owner coupe for US$28.50. I did 5000 miles [8047 km] in it and made a profit of US$10 when I sold it.

I was walking along a street in Torrance [south-western Los Angeles] with Elby Stuart's daughter. I was on the lookout for a car, and said, 'That little black Chevvy would be handy if you knew who owned it.' The owner turned out to be a fellow cleaning the car. I said, 'I understand that's your Chevvy, sir. Do you want to sell it?' He said it had been sitting there for three months and he wasn't sure if it would go. We got it going, and he took me for a drive. He asked me how would $30 suit me, and it suited me fine. When I was cleaning it I found an additional spare tyre that didn't fit the car, so I sold it for $1.50, which brought the car price down to $28.50.

I drove on highway US 101 to the Redwood Highway, then over the mountains to Redding, then down through Sacramento, the Imperial Valley in south-east California, and on to Mexico. I was heading for Mexico City when, about 200 miles [322 km] from Tijuana, the Mexican police ordered me out of the country because I didn't have a proper visa. I travelled round for about a week then headed for Las Vegas.

I then spent a couple of days at the Boulder Dam, and then in Boulder City saw a film about its construction. From there, I headed back to Los Angeles, then on to San Francisco, where I stayed a week before selling the car for $38.50. That 1940 Chev coupe had 70,000 miles [112,654 km] on the clock. It had chrome fittings over the dashboard. The model that was sold in New Zealand had plastic fittings. A day or two after I sold the car, I caught the ship to New Zealand.

When I came home I worked on the bike through the year. I still didn't intend taking it to the United States. I could still ride on the road at Swannanoa in Canterbury in those days.

[Long, straight South Island roads were often used for motorcycle speed events. Modern health and safety regulations make it difficult to get a road closed for such events. You now need a traffic-management plan, including detour routes. Then there may well be objections from livestock owners, especially those with horses, because they fear the noise will spook their animals.]

Chapter 8
SECOND US TRIP, 1957: YEAR OF THE PLYMOUTH

Again I went to America without the bike. This time I left the ship at San Francisco. I went to San Jose to look at older cars. Back in San Francisco, an African-American, Joe, I met there on my first trip, owned a specialist transmission outfit.

'You're back from Australia — no, Noo Zealand,' he greeted me.

I told Joe that in San Jose I hadn't found anything without a big mileage. He mentioned a Plymouth, and arranged for me to see it. It was a one-owner 1940 Plymouth light sedan, and I bought it for US$105.

Here's a warning to anyone buying a car. The Plymouth ran like new as I drove around San Francisco hills, and 200 miles [322 km] later I found out why. I didn't know it had 3X supplement in the engine oil. This, at a cost of about $3, fills up the spaces between worn parts, but after a few hundred miles disappears. I got under the car and put in a set of Mobil bearing shelves, then I set off for New York.

I went to Salt Lake City for a few days, then visited Denver. I drove down to Dodge City, Kansas, and visited Boot Hill, where the gunmen are buried.

[Boot Hill was the name for many Western American towns' cemeteries for gunfighters, who were said to die with their boots on. Dodge City's is one of the more famous Boot Hills.]

I spent three days at the Dodge City motorbike races. Riders come there from all over the United States, particularly for the half-mile [0.8 km] and the drag, or standing quarter-mile [0.4 km]. They are much better riders than in New Zealand. Their blood seems to be redder.

In Invercargill we had a dirt track and the lap record was about 20 seconds for the quarter-mile. The half-mile tracks in America, such as Ascot Speedway, near Gardena, Los Angeles [closed in 1990], had a record under 23 seconds, but for the half-mile. The Yanks ride tracks like road racers. The surface is usually shale, much harder than cinders. There is very little loose stuff. It's hair-raising, and more riders get killed than on the dirt tracks in New Zealand, Australia and Europe.

[In 2014, Dodge City marked the centennial of its famous 300-mile (482.8-km) world championship on a two-mile (3.2-km) dirt oval. In the 1950s, the big race was usually over 100 miles (160.9 km), but in 1957, the year of Burt's visit, it was 75 miles (120.7 km). The winner was Al Gunter on a Harley-Davidson.]

Leaving Dodge City, I had an unusual experience. I met people who invited me to visit them in Kansas City. I rarely picked anyone up, but I saw two young girls who looked harmless enough and who seemed to want a ride badly. I said, 'Hop in.' I asked them where they were going and it was exactly the address of my first call, a motorcycle shop. They were thinking of buying an Indian Chief, but I advised them to buy a lightweight bike.

BEFORE I LEFT DODGE CITY, I got sinus trouble so bad, so painful, I couldn't stand vibration, and couldn't take the wheel off to fix a puncture. A man who helped me suggested I go to a medical clinic. I waited hours to see a doctor. When he found I was from New Zealand, he wanted to talk about the New Zealand deer he had heard about. He wanted to visit our country to hunt. Finally, I had to say, 'What about my head?' The doctor said I had Mid-West sinus. Driving through dry air had dried out my sinuses. He gave me US$12 worth of spray and tablets. I took them until I was somewhere near Detroit.

I travelled on, visiting factories when I could. I was still taking the tablets and using the spray. At three o'clock one morning I awoke and felt that I was dying. I was saturated with sweat. I thought, 'If I don't get to a doctor pretty quick I will be a dead duck.' I couldn't stand upright as I struggled into the car. I asked at a gas station where the nearest hospital was. The attendant got a taxi to accompany me to the hospital.

They put me to bed at 4 a.m. Tests indicated I should stay in hospital. They told me it would cost $40 a day. I exploded, 'Forty dollars a day!' They kept taking checks and at 6 a.m. the doctor came back and said he had rung a specialist, and I should be dead, but now my temperature had dropped. I said, 'If I'm going to die, I might as well die in the old Plymouth.' I got dressed and went out to the car. The doctor just looked. He didn't make me pay.

I drove on, heading for Chicago. I talked to a guy on the road who told me I was on the right road. I kept going straight for about 100 miles [161 km]. I thought I should be able to see some tall buildings, but I couldn't. I stopped at a service station. The guy told me I was in Indiana. My head was so bad I couldn't fix a punctured tyre. The man in the gas station mended it for me, and wouldn't take a penny. After this I headed in the right direction. I had a sleeping bag, and sometimes slept in the car parked on a quiet side road, but not when I was in the big cities. I always ate at diners.

I spent three days on the road, including a run to Milwaukee to visit the factory of Harley-Davidson, the only American motorcycle maker apart from Indian to survive the Depression. I got to Harley-Davidson on a Saturday and was shown through the factory. It was a very big operation, and they were building a second factory at the time. The existing factory was bigger than any motorcycle factory I had visited in England. It had about half an acre [0.2 hectares] of bikes in a dispatch room, and they said none left unless they had a firm order for them.

I remember asking a fellow, 'Why don't you build bikes smaller, like Triumphs and Velocettes — they weigh about 800 pounds [363 kg]?'

He said, 'The guys won't have them any other way.'

I HEADED BACK TO CHICAGO, with the aim of visiting Detroit. On the way, I pulled up behind a big inter-state truck and had a snooze. There was a crossroad with a stop light. Another big truck was slowing about 200 yards [183 metres] away. When the light changed, I moved out and followed the big truck. We moved up to 70 miles per hour [112.7 km/h]. Two miles [3.2 km] further on, the police stopped me. A cop started to write me a ticket, saying I had pulled out in front of the truck. I hadn't. I explained, and he said he was giving me a warning ticket, and if I got another one I would go into the 'cooler'.

In Detroit, I visited Ford's River Rouge plant at Dearborn. Fifty-four thousand people worked there, and the plant was so big it had its own bus service. I saw the processes from manufacturing parts to final painting.

I then set off for Toronto, but the Canadian border officials wanted something called the 'pink slip' before they would let me take the car across. I found the receipt for its purchase, but that wasn't enough, so I stored the car and went to Toronto — and back — by bus.

Then I left for Toledo and Cleveland back in the United States. I nearly lost the car in Toledo. I had a flat tyre, and jacked the car up at a gas station. It slid off the jack. As it began to go over I yelled to a guy at the gas station, and we got it right again.

I spent a day in Cleveland, looking at the big tool factories. Around this Lake Erie area I took ill and nearly died, with a temperature so low a man shouldn't live at all, but after three hours I got up and drove on.

In Buffalo, I was looking for a parking area when I saw a place, all parking meters. You backed in and you paid five cents for an hour. When I came back to the car, there was a red ticket in the window. There was no parking there from 11 a.m. to 4 p.m. There was a guy checking the cars, and I told him I didn't see any warning. He said there was a notice on a pole down the street someplace. I said, 'I don't feel like paying the two dollars.' He looked at my car's California licence plate and said it was a long way to California. 'By God you're right,' I said, and I still owe the city of Buffalo two dollars. As I drove away, cars parked for two or three blocks had red stickers on them.

I visited Niagara Falls, floodlit at night with coloured lights, and with beautiful gardens and buildings round about. Lots of honeymooners were mooning about. Next day, I drove to Chicago, then headed for Springfield, Massachusetts, where the Indian Motocycle Company factory used to be. On the way, I navigated through Albany, New York, which has the worst traffic laws in the world. They had you down to about 10 miles per hour [16.1 km/h].

FINALLY, I GOT TO SPRINGFIELD. I went straight to the factory. I began to break out in perspiration, as I was getting another attack of illness. The factory was closed. It had been sold out three years earlier, in 1954. I parked the car and went into a supermarket to get a drink of water. A girl gave me one, and I went out and over the street to a fire station. It was summer, and the engines were sitting out in the open. The firemen let me sit on an easy chair. One said, 'You don't look so well.' I asked where I could find a doctor, and they pointed across the street. By this time, I couldn't stand up. A fireman each got under an arm and they helped me across to a Dr Tauber.

The girl at reception said, 'Sorry, it's 5 p.m. and we're shut.' However, she looked over to the firemen and got the doctor, and after examining me he said, 'Munro, I don't know what's the matter with you.' I suggested it might be the side effect of the tablet I was taking for my sinus problem. The doctor told me to spend the night in a hotel, and gave me his number for them to ring him if I got worse. I improved by morning. I kept taking the spray for my sinuses, but stopped taking the tablets, and had no more attacks. The sinus trouble began going away after a month.

Next day, I heard the Indian factory had a downtown development workshop and office. I found it, and gave my name at the desk. Paul Hill, then the manager, came out, read my name, then introduced me to half a dozen other men.

'We've heard a lot about your machine. We probably know more about it than you do,' Paul said.

I hadn't written about it myself, but apparently a lot of people had. In those days I held a New Zealand open record of 143.3 miles per hour [230.6 km/h], an under 750 cc record, and beach records. I talked to them for a couple of hours, then they lined me up with racing equipment and took photographs and movies. They gave me a factory racing jersey, four club jerseys, T-shirts, and the only 1928-design Indian crankpin they had.

I was very disappointed. For 30 years, it had been my ambition to visit the factory, and when I got there it was closed. The old owners had died, and others had sold their shares. The company went downhill. In the old days, their bikes were the best in the world. Their best bike was the 1928 Super Scout, or the 101 as it was known in America. A friend had one in mint condition, and turned down an offer of US$1200 for it.

I said goodbye to the Indian people, and set off for Boston. For a few years, I got Christmas cards from Paul Hill.

[Indian production ended in 1953, when the company went broke. Brockhouse Engineering acquired rights to the Indian name and until 1960 they imported English Royal Enfield motorcycles, mildly customised them, and sold them as Indians. In 1960, the Indian name was bought by AMC of England, a competitor of Royal Enfield. The goal was to sell Matchless and AJS motorcycles badged as Indians. AMC itself went into liquidation in 1962. As this is written in 2015, Indian Motorcycle Company is back in business, but now with the 'r' in its official name. This time, Indian is a subsidiary of Polaris Industries, the American company that is a world leader in snowmobiles and all-terrain vehicles or ATVs.]

IN BOSTON, I SAW THE Paul Revere monument, then pressed on to New York. I headed for a hotel in 112th Street and stayed for three days at US$2.50 a day. It was a big room with wall-to-wall carpet and reading lamps.

The first night, I thought I would walk to Times Square. I walked about ten blocks and came across a crowd outside a small, old building. I asked what had happened.

'They've shot a guy in there,' a man said. 'I've been here half an hour and the police haven't been here yet.'

Then there were sirens as police arrived in cars and on motorcycles. They went in and brought out an African-American woman kicking and screaming. Early next morning, I read a newspaper. The incident wasn't even mentioned.

I spent three days in New York, and was nearly arrested. I was headed for 112th Street and asked people whether I was going the right way. I was, but they said over the bridge there's no through traffic on this block — it's a children's play area. I didn't see any children, so I thought, 'Oh hell, I'm going through.' At the other end the police nabbed me. I was able to talk my way out of a charge.

Next day I went out to Floyd Bennett Field, New York's first municipal airport, then to Idlewild Airport [renamed John F. Kennedy International Airport in 1963]. On the way, I got tangled in a traffic jam. A big, plutocratic-looking guy in a convertible was jammed next to me. I yelled to him, asking if I was on the right way to Idlewild Airport. He said yes, then noticed my California licence plates. He had visited California, and had a great time there.

'When we get moving, pull in and I'll help you.'

He led me five miles [8 km] along an overhead highway, then through a parkway. I got to Idlewild, but it took about two hours. Coming back, I followed the crowd and I seemed to get back in about three quarters of an hour.

FROM NEW YORK, I DROVE south on US Route 11. I was greatly taken by the housing style in Philadelphia, then headed to Baltimore for a day, before going to Washington. I visited the 554-feet 7.3-inches [169 metres] tall Washington monument, the Lincoln Memorial, Arlington cemetery, the Pentagon, and the other great buildings of the American capital.

Then I drove on until the car blew up 45 miles [72.4 km]

south of Washington. I heard a wee ting-ting under the bonnet [hood], but drove another quarter of a mile [400 metres] to a gas station. The water pump had failed and let all the water out. The head was cracked right across and right down one side. The pinging was the expansion pressure coming out.

The gas station was shut, but I walked two miles [3.2 km] down a side road to where the owner lived. His wife answered the door. He had gone fishing. I walked back the two miles, and decided to try another bit of radiator powder. In five minutes I was bowling down the highway for the first of 6000 miles [9656 km] with 40 cents of powder in the water. It fixed, too, the water pump, which had been leaking. The water was that hot you didn't notice the engine getting hot.

I headed for Roanoke, Virginia. Next morning I was just going to pass a woman going slow in a lane, when she stopped suddenly and I hit her back fender. I got her to pull over to the side and said I was willing to fix any damage, but she said her husband would take care of it.

I found I had missed the Gettysburg battle site, but I visited several other Civil War sites, beginning with Manassas Junction, where the two Bull Run battles were fought. Others I visited on my trip included Missionary Ridge and Vicksburg. They all had big bronze monuments. Tears ran down my cheeks at times, they were so sad. The people in those days had so much feeling for the casualties. In the Hitler war, at times people could barely raise the money to add to monuments the names of casualties. The South was still recovering from the war, as far as I could see. There were many old houses and many neglected farms.

I reached Birmingham, Alabama, perhaps best known for its steel industry — I visited the big steel works at the nearby town of Bessemer — and almost had a bad crash. I was on the main route through the city and never saw some lights. The red was against me, but I drove straight through. I just missed a guy in a big car who had the right of way.

When I reached Meridian, Mississippi, I blew the car up

again. I wrecked another piston. It was early in the morning and I spoke to two African-American girls, aged about 20 or 22, right at a sharp turn in the street where I had to slow down. I asked them if they could tell me where downtown was. When I spoke to them, they got such a shock they looked at each other and almost ran for their lives. They never spoke. I had already noted picnic rest areas on the highways in the South were either for 'white' people or for 'coloured' people. At bus stops, facilities for African-Americans were upstairs, and for whites they were downstairs.

I found a garage the owner let me use all day while it rained continuously. He lent me tools and got me a piston at cost price. I did the whole repair job that day and left next morning. I had planned to head for New Orleans, but a check on my finances soon ruled this out. I drove to Vicksburg on the Mississippi River, then pulled up in Tallulah, across the river in Louisiana. I parked the car at a gas station and walked across the highway to a diner. When I came back, an old guy was changing a tyre.

'Got a flat there?' I asked.

'What state are you from, young fellow?' he asked. I was 58.

I told him I was a foreigner, and he gave me fatherly advice: don't pick up strangers. In 1928, the gas station owner asked a man if he was headed to St Louis, because two men at the station wanted a lift. Asked whether he knew them, the gas station man said they had been round 'quite a bit'. So they got a ride to St Louis. They lay in the back seats and slept until it was dark. The car driver woke up four days later in hospital. The pair waited until he stopped and slept in the front, then dragged him out of the car, beat him, and left him on the road. The police picked the pair up from his description, and they both were sentenced to 20 years in prison and died there. There are so many murders in the United States that I seldom picked up anyone.

In Louisiana it struck me that wherever I stopped, black beetles up to an inch [2.5 cm] big crawled over the ground at night. They used to give me the creeps, but locals didn't take any notice of them.

To save money, I headed for Texas and Mexico in place of New Orleans. I drove towards Dallas and Fort Worth. I visited the Will Rogers Memorial Center in Fort Worth and visited a lot of motorcycle shops in both cities. I had been invited to visit Pete Dalio's Triumph in Dallas.

[In 1954 Dalio, airline pilot Stormy Mangham and mechanic Jack Wilson rebuilt a Triumph as the 'Devil's Arrow' to challenge NSU for the world motorcycle record. Mangham tested their streamliner design on his DC-6 airliner, outside the cockpit window. In September 1956, Johnny Allen rode the machine across the Bonneville Salt Flats, setting an absolute speed record of 193.7 mph (311.7 km/h), but FIM, the international motorcycling organisation, refused to ratify it.]

I went out to visit Mangham's private airfield. They entertained me all day at Fort Worth, and took me out to dinner. They loaded me up with T-shirts, and Pete Dalio T-shirts are hard to come by.

The biggest oil well ever drilled was being sunk at Fort Stockton, 130 miles [209 km] off my route, and I wanted to see it. On the way to the drilling project, I saw a pick-up truck in the distance on a lonely road, in desert country. Five suspicious-looking characters pushed the truck a bit when they saw me coming, and I couldn't get past it without going off the road, where there was a bank. I was forced to stop.

The pick-up truck was running on propane, a cheap fuel. I asked where they were from and they said Fort Stockton. They had run out of gas, and I figured they had stolen the vehicle. They wanted me to turn my car around and drive them to Monahans, about 50 to 60 miles [80.5 to 96.6 km] back along the road. I had my window down about four inches [10 cm] talking to them, and they came from the front round to the side. They were really suspicious-looking, and I thought they might steal my car. I nicked the car into gear as I began, 'I'll tell you what I'll do. The first car I meet coming this way . . .' Then I was off, and I haven't seen them since.

I got to the drilling site 13 miles [20.9 km] out of Fort Stockton, but they told me I wasn't allowed on-site. While I was being tackled about this, a geologist who lived in a caravan on-site told me the drill bit down four miles [6.4 km] at a time. The geologist asked me why I had parked my car 200 yards [182.9 metres] from the derrick. I told him I thought they might strike a gusher. He laughed and declared me a guest of the project. He said the derrick was as big as any in the world.

Before midnight they let me, for a minute or two, control the drill. There was a big brake-band arrangement that held the weight of the drill. It had a big dial — about six feet across [1.8 metres] — that registered tonnage. I was holding 150 US tons [136 metric tonnes]. They were drilling 70 feet [21.3 metres], then hauling out a four-mile [6.4-km] pipe and putting on new cutters. It took 14 hours. A length of the drill pipe, 200 feet [61 metres], was stacked inside the derrick. The drill started at 17 inches [43.2 cm] diameter then went down to 7.5 inches [19 cm], then, I think, smaller again.

The drilling had been going non-stop for 18 months. A year later I read a story in a magazine about it. They had gone down to 25,300 feet [7.7 km] — then the deepest drilled in the world. The drill cost US$10 million. I asked the geologist, 'Who pays for all this?' He said the University of Texas did. The drill was on the fringe of the oil area of Texas. You could smell oil in the air all day long. The university had been given many mile-square [259-hectare] sections there.

FROM THE BIG RIG, I drove to El Paso, where I stayed several days. I made day trips into Mexico. I topped up each time with

A 1920 Indian Scout motorcycle on display in the Reynolds-Alberta Museum in Wetaskiwin, Alberta, Canada. REYNOLDS-ALBERTA MUSEUM

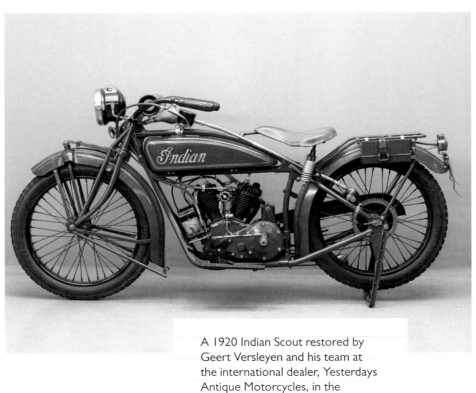

A 1920 Indian Scout restored by Geert Versleyen and his team at the international dealer, Yesterdays Antique Motorcycles, in the Netherlands. WWW.YESTERDAYS.NL

Burt at Oreti Beach races in 1929.
MUNRO FAMILY COLLECTION

Burt on the Indian Scout in 1928.
MUNRO FAMILY COLLECTION

Burt pushes the Indian to 125 mph (201.16 kph) in a run on Otaitai Beach, Southland, in 1953. MUNRO FAMILY COLLECTION

The Munro Special — number 18 instead of the later 35 — on soft sand at Oreti Beach in 1949. E. HAYES MOTORWORKS COLLECTION

In this photo taken in the 1960s, Burt Munro obliges a photographer for a picture on his beloved Indian Scout, which was by this time more than 40 years old. DONALD BUCKLEY PHOTOGRAPHICS

This is how Burt Munro often transported his motorcycles: he towed them. Burt and friend Alf Groves at Oreti Beach in the early 1960s. E. HAYES MOTORWORKS COLLECTION

Bound for Grants Pass, Oregon, Burt changes the oil in the 1948 Pontiac Hydra-Matic straight-eight in this photo taken in 1959. This was the favourite of the cars he drove on his North American tours. MUNRO FAMILY COLLECTION

During petrol rationing in World War II, Burt made a coal-gas unit for the motorcycle he used as a travelling salesman. Front and back views. MUNRO FAMILY COLLECTION

Burt at his beloved Myford lathe. He wore it out and rebuilt it three times.

DONALD BUCKLEY PHOTOGRAPHICS

The evolution of the streamliner for Burt's Indian Scout motorcycle begins. The removed side panel shows how Burt crouched inside the shell.
MUNRO FAMILY COLLECTION

The streamliner, with its triple-fin tail, outside Burt Munro's workshop-home.
E. HAYES MOTORWORKS COLLECTION

Shown here in 1963, the third version of the streamliner, this time with a single-fin tail. From left, a young Neville Hayes, Burt, Norman Hayes (Neville's father) and Stuart Varley (Norman's brother-in-law). E. HAYES MOTORWORKS COLLECTION

Enthusiasts at Bonneville in August 1962 presented Burt with a bag of dollars to mark his record run.
GETTY IMAGES

Irving Hayes, Burt Munro's Invercargill friend and backer, with the 1939 Dodge he drove in saloon-car beach races and hill climbs. (New Zealand saloon-car racing is similar to stock-car racing in North America. New Zealand stock cars have rigid steel guards, and full contact between vehicles is encouraged.) E. HAYES MOTORWORKS COLLECTION

Burt making a run on the Salt Flats at Bonneville in 1962.
GETTY IMAGES

Burt prepares for a record run at Bonneville in 1962. GETTY IMAGES

In this photo taken at Bonneville in 1966, Burt works on the Indian while, in the background, sits the Alex Tremulis-designed Gyronaut X-1 — a scene that struck the photographer as a juxtaposition of old and new technologies.
GETTY IMAGES

Burt prepares for his last run at Bonneville in 1971. Flame-proof trousers weren't enough to exempt him from tough new streamliner rules.
RICHARD MENZIES

Burt being pushed off at the start of his final run on the Salt Flats in 1971. New rules forced him to take off the streamliner shell. RICHARD MENZIES

The end: Burt after his final run on the Salt Flats in 1971. RICHARD MENZIES

Burt in October 1973, at age 74, riding his Velocette in the Alexandra Motorcycling Club's quarter-mile sprints on the Galloway Straight, just outside Alexandra, Central Otago.
DAVID WETHEY

Burt's Velocette as it might have looked when new. This 1936 500-cc Velocette has been restored by a British enthusiast. VELOCETTE OWNERS CLUB, BRITAIN

Inspired by the film *The World's Fastest Indian*, Leslie Porterfield of Texas has set world records at Bonneville. LESLIE PORTERFIELD

A new Indian Scout. American manufacturer Polaris Industries has revived Indian Motorcycle manufacturing.

Clockwise from top: pistons, a camshaft and a conrod from the Indian Scout.

FRANK KLETSCHKUS

Clockwise from top: Burt's Velocette and Indian Scout on display at E. Hayes and Son, Invercargill; Burt's tombstone in Invercargill; the Indian Scout's engine. FRANK KLETSCHKUS

Clockwise from top: Riders spin through soft sand as they race on Oreti Beach in Invercargill's annual Burt Munro Challenge rally. SOUTHLAND TIMES, FAIRFAX NZ; Invercargill's statue of Burt Munro on his Indian Scout in the city's Gala Street reserve. Sculpted by Roddy McMillan, the statue was completed in 2011. ASH; Invercargill Mayor Tim Shadbolt, in full civic regalia, gets into the spirit of the Burt Munro Challenge. SOUTHLAND TIMES, FAIRFAX NZ petrol at 20 cents a US gallon [about 5 cents a litre]. Lots of young men would spring to and polish the windscreen. I found later I was supposed to tip them.

Across the Rio Grande from El Paso, in Ciudad Juárez, driving was on dirt roads. The footpaths were dirt, and the people were very poor. A Mexican barber cut my hair at a regular price of US20 cents, but I paid him double. On the United States side of the river a haircut cost US$1.75. Many prettier Mexican girls who could speak English worked in stores in El Paso.

I was on my way to Mexico City down a big highway when the police stopped me. I told them I was on my way to Mexico City.

'No you're not,' they said. 'You're heading right back out of here, pronto.'

I had no visa.

I spent a week back in the Texas border area, then headed for Alamogordo, New Mexico, where the first atomic bomb test was held in 1945. [The Manhattan Project's Trinity test on 16 July 1945. The site is now part of a US Army missile range.] I wasn't allowed on the site, because it was still radioactive. The test vaporised a steel tower, and left a sheet of glass about 20 inches [50.8 cm] thick and 600 feet [182.9 metres] in diameter.

I headed back to Las Cruces, New Mexico, just a small desert town. [Las Cruces now has more than 100,000 people, and is the second-largest city in New Mexico.] I fell in love with the New Mexico desert country. I wouldn't mind living there. The yucca trees — a sort of cactus — the reddish soil, the fantastically steep mountains, the great open stretches. I headed over to Silver City, where there had been a lot of silver mining in the early days, then headed north, picking up a hitch-hiker. Then I drove into Arizona, to Holbrook. I turned the hitch-hiker down the first time, then met him at a diner 150 miles [241.4 km] further on. He was looking for work, so I picked him up this time.

Travelling through an Arizona forest I saw the biggest stag I had seen in my life. Some hunters would have given their left testicle to shoot it.

--------35--------

THEN I WAS AT FLAGSTAFF, Arizona, and on to Williams, on famous Route 66. From Williams it is about 60 miles [96.6 km] to the Grand Canyon. By the time I had got 12 miles [19.3 km] from Williams, the car was going so badly I thought it would blow to bits. I drove into some bush on the side of the highway. I drove it into the scrub until it wouldn't go another inch.

In the morning, I got up early and found my way to a junk yard. It opened at 6 a.m., and I said I wanted another piston for a 1940 model Plymouth. We hunted all round and couldn't find any, then I saw what turned out to be one. It was sitting on a rail. It was brand new — it had never been used. It had been sitting on the rail in the yard, and was brown with age. It was in the yard's price book at $6.80, but I asked, 'Who are you going to sell it to?' They gave it to me for $3.40.

I was able to drive the car to a garage in Williams, a town of 2000 or 3000 people. Some guys in the garage loaned me tools and let me work there. I worked until 9 p.m. without anything to eat. I took four of the six pistons out. Apart from the new one, I had installed another earlier on the trip, at Meridian. I sawed round every ring and groove to widen it evenly, then fitted spacer rings to take up the gap. After 9 p.m., I got cleaned up then went along and had a great dinner. On the trip, I always had bacon and eggs for breakfast. You used to get two fried eggs, toast and jelly [jam] for 55 cents. I don't remember the price of bacon.

The garage was open all night. The town was on one side, and on the other side were beautiful mountains. On the way from the diner to the garage, a tough-looking character with a growth of beard asked me for 50 cents. He scared me, but I asked him to give me a dollar instead. When I reached the garage, I mentioned the man to the three mechanics who worked at night selling petrol and doing repairs.

'Where is he?' one asked. When I told him he was round the corner, he phoned the police.

Soon a deputy sheriff arrived and quizzed me about the fellow. The deputy suspected he might be a desperado they were seeking in the hills to charge with murder. From my description, however, they decided he was no bandit.

THE GRAND CANYON PROVED TO be fantastic — the size and age of it. There's a Harley-Davidson at the bottom of it. Went down, and couldn't get back up. It's still there.

Then I headed for the Boulder Dam, driving through Kingman. I stayed the night at Boulder City, and went back to the dam next day. I went on a tour through the dam, and had a swim in the lake. At that time it was the highest dam in the world, with the lake-top water 550 feet [167.6 metres] above water on the down side of the dam.

I never drove at night. I didn't want to miss seeing anything. By now I was finding it tough going, sleeping in the back of the car. Earlier on, I often stayed at motels, where the summer price was $18 a night without food.

From Boulder City I pressed on to Las Vegas. I had been there before, but never stayed long. I decided to do some gambling. It was really hot. I was in the habit of travelling just in shoes and slacks. Early on, I was in a club without a shirt. A girl asked me to put on a shirt. I thought she was having me on, but one of the house police said, 'Sorry, but she means it.' I went out and got a white shirt, then the guy showed me how to work the machines.

I played slot machines at the Million Dollar Club and at the

Golden Nugget, and saw some of the top entertainers. Las Vegas is a tremendous place, with tremendous lighting and wide open spaces. I spent a day there gambling, and was down only $2 at the end of the day, but my arms were aching.

Then I set off for Los Angeles. I coasted 18 miles [29 km] in neutral on downgrades in the high country. I mainly kept to 60 miles per hour [96.6 km/h]. I stopped at Baker and filled empty oil cans with water, ready to take the old car into Death Valley in the Mojave Desert [the lowest, driest and hottest area in North America]. At the gas station, they advised me not to go into Death Valley. They said it was 125 degrees to 130 degrees every day [51.7 to 54.4 degrees Celsius].

'If your car breaks go down you'll be dehydrated in 30 hours,' one man said.

I drove on. I got to 60 miles [96.6 km] in, just before Shoshone Village, and the car was boiling badly. I stopped on top of a rise. The Plymouth boiled for 10 minutes by my watch. I wanted to put more water in and got impatient, even into a bit of rage. I undid the filler cap and a geyser of red, dusty water shot up four feet [1.2 metres]. It emptied the radiator. I poured a little water on the block and waited a long time to get the heat down. Then I headed further into the desert.

I got to Furnace Creek [a tiny resort with two hotels that were operating when Burt was there] about two o'clock in the afternoon with the temperature about 130 degrees [54.4 degrees Celsius]. It was about 280 feet [85.3 metres] below sea level. It was a thousand miles [1609 km] since I changed the oil. It was time to change.

I drove the car up so the drain plug would be downhill, and drained the oil. I got the new oil in, but then couldn't start her. I managed to get the car out onto the road with the electric starter. There was a bit of a downgrade going the opposite way to where I was going. Thinking of the water and the heat, I pushed like mad going downhill, jumped in, got the car into gear, but it wouldn't fire.

I checked the ignition, and found the main wire had come out of the distributor. Going again, I headed for Scotty's Castle, also known as Death Valley Ranch.

[Death Valley Ranch was built as a holiday getaway by a wealthy couple, Albert and Bessie Johnson, but Walter Scott, or Death Valley Scotty, had everyone believe he built the castle with money from secret mines he claimed to have in the desert.]

I got to the castle, and it cost two or three dollars to be shown the place. I said I was a long way from home and couldn't afford that. When they found out I was from overseas they let me in free.

I slept in the car and had another look around the place in the morning. In a shed were some vintage cars, including a 1908 Stutz. On a small hill near the castle was the grave of Scotty, who died about three years before. A searchlight played on the tombstone at night. I went up to look at the grave, and was on the lookout for rattlesnakes when I caught a spider, about five inches [12.7 cm] across. It was a young tarantula. I caught it alive and put it in a beer can, and kept him in the back of the car. Next day, though, it was dead.

ON THE WAY OUT OF Death Valley I headed for the small settlement of Baker, in the Mojave Desert, then on to Bakersfield, a city in the San Joaquin Valley, 110 miles [177 km] north of Los Angeles.

When I arrived in Los Angeles, the first thing I wanted to do was get a new head and two new pistons for the Plymouth. I went to an acquaintance in Lawndale, in the South Bay area of Los Angeles. He remembered me from the previous visit, when I had the Chevvy. He asked what he could do to help, and when I said I had a cracked head on the Plymouth he said,

'Go down and see my brother.'

'From Australia?' asked the brother.

'No, from New Zealand,' I said.

He shook my hand and said he had been stationed in New Zealand in the Second World War, and had been 'treated fine'.

He showed me an engine and gearbox, completely reconditioned with all new parts, a new water pump, a new fan belt and coil, new wiring, and rebored over-size with new pistons — and it had never been run. I asked the price of the head, and he said 50 cents. I got the head off, and he came across and asked how I got the head off, and said, 'Aren't you taking the crankshaft?'

'What? For 50 cents?'

'Yes,' he replied, so for 50 cents he let me strip the whole engine.

I HAD A WEEK OR two left before I sailed to New Zealand, so I headed up Route 99 to San Francisco and met friends I made at the Salt on my previous trip. On that first trip I went up Route 101.

[Route 99 was the main north–south numbered highway on the US West Coast until 1964. It was sometimes called the Main Street of California. Route 101 remains, but the main north–south link is Interstate 5 Highway.]

I met the widow of Lloyd 'Sprouts' Elder, the rider I had known in Australia. He had just died at Fresno, so I called to offer my condolences. [Elder died in 1957, so it must have been only months before Burt's meeting with Mrs Elder.] Then I headed to Oakland, the port just east of San Francisco, on San Francisco Bay. I planned to ship the Plymouth back to New Zealand, but they said it would cost me $600. I drove it to a junk yard and offered it to them. Normally they would have paid only a few dollars for it, but they finally offered me $75 — and a job as salesman. I turned down both offers and went to another place, where I got $80 for her. With the money I stayed in a hotel for a week, then caught the *Orsova* home.

On the trip I covered 11,000 miles [17,702 km].

I WAS HOME IN INVERCARGILL from 1957 to 1959, working on the Indian all the time. I kept trying to win the two-mile [3.2-km] dash, but each year something would blow up.

To jump back a year, Southland, my home province, celebrated its centennial in 1956. I was at a meeting of the Southland Motorcycle Club in the Automobile Association rooms when they were trying to get competitors for a centennial road race at Ryal Bush. They asked me if I would enter. My bike wasn't suitable, but if I had a foot-gear-shift machine I would give it a go. Next day, a guy came to my place and said he had heard I was looking for a bike to run in a road race.

'I've got a 1936 Velocette you can have for two years, then I'll call back for it,' he told me.

I said I would think about it.

Next day I went over and picked it up and pulled it apart. It was such a mess. Everything was broken. Even the magneto was broken in half.

The owner came a few days later. 'Is the deal on?' he asked.

'No,' I told him. 'If I work on it I'll be the owner.'

So I bought it from him there and then for five pounds [$10].

[George Begg writes, however, in *Burt Munro: Indian Legend of Speed*, that Burt and a friend, Percy Shave, bought two rusted 500 cc MSS Velocettes that lay in a shed at Nightcaps.

They bought the pair for ten pounds — $20 — then flipped a coin and Burt got the 1936 model. These models were built as touring bikes, initially in 1935. A new model was launched after World War II. Begg concludes that, from information from the head of the English Velocette Owners Club, the speed Burt eventually achieved with this machine — 142 miles per hour (228.5 km/h) — made it the world's fastest Velocette. Begg writes that, for years, scrawled on the Velocette's petrol tank was the name '5 pound special'.]

I worked on the Velocette for two or three months. I got it going and took it out for the first test run on Oreti Beach in 1957. I got three miles [4.8 km] down the beach before it seized up in the exhaust valve guide. It damaged a piston and had to be rebuilt. Since then it has blown up another 61 times over 10 years. The Velocette is 491 cc, short stroke.

In February 1961, I rode the Velo in a six-mile [9.7-km] open handicap. I did it in four minutes 18.6 seconds — 83.4 miles per hour [134.2 km/h]. In March 1962, I set the New Zealand standing quarter-mile [402.3 metres] record for the open class on it in a time of 12.31 seconds. My best performance, 135.6 miles per hour [218.2 km/h], was in a one-way run over a flying half-mile [804.7 metres].

I made dozens of pistons for the Velocette [and increased the capacity to over 600 cc]. I made two crankcase halves, titanium cam followers, and a dozen or more steel piston rods. In the Ryal Bush centennial race, the competition included riders like Mick Holland and Tom McCleary, from Christchurch. The Velocette seized up in the second lap. It was the exhaust valve again. I rode in the Southbridge road race near Christchurch about 1958 or 1959, and split the tank in the third lap. I also rode in the New Zealand Grand Prix several times.

The Southbridge race followed a record number of blow-ups in a few days. I test-tuned the bike at Oreti Beach on the

Thursday night before the weekend race, and wrecked the back end. I worked all night and rebuilt it, and a friend and I left home at 3 a.m. I hadn't been to bed. We got to Geraldine and rested at a hotel.

We hadn't time for a proper test run, so in the morning we tested her on a quiet road. There was a hole in the piston. I took the bike to a friend's place in Christchurch. He had no welding plant, so I bored a little hole in the centre of the piston. Both friends said that if I tapped the hole out and put in a plug, and riveted it over inside and outside, it would hold.

We went out on Sunday to Tram Road, north of Christchurch, where we shouldn't have been.

[Tram Road is a 10-mile (16.1-km stretch) of long, straight road about 22 miles (35.4 km) north of Christchurch that was often used for racing. On Tram Road in 1955, another Invercargill motorcyclist, Russel Wright, riding a Vincent Black Lightning, set a world record for motorcycles, averaging 184.83 mph (297.45 km/h) in two runs. Russel as a teenager would visit Burt in his shack-workshop, and it was there that he caught the speed bug. Russel died aged 83 in 2013. His ashes were scattered along Tram Road, as he wished.]

I went back about three miles [4.8 km] from a crossroad, where my two friends were waiting. I was going to shut off before I got to them. The Velocette was going beautifully, whining more like a 300 cc than a 500 cc. Just as I was about to shut off, it suddenly melted the piston, and started to leak fuel.

We went back to McLeary's Garage, run by a friend. It had a welding plant, but no welding rod, and by this time there was a downpour of rain. It was any port in a storm. We fished around in the dark out the back of the garage and found an old piston. I sawed it into strips in the garage and welded it into one long strip for a welding rod.

We went out to the Grand Prix next day. I had missed

practice on the Saturday, so I went out for the big race without a test run. Because I missed the practice, they put me in the Rangiora Handicap to see how the bike was going. This was before the Grand Prix. There were about 70 riders, and I remember passing a lot of bikes. In the last lap, I was out in front with about five miles [8 km] to go when the exhaust valve broke off. It knocked a hole in the piston valve about 1.5 inches [3.8 cm] across.

From the Thursday night to the end of the Rangiora Handicap the Velocette had four blow-ups.

IN 1951, I DID 110.43 miles per hour [177.7 km/h] on the Indian to take the national flying open beach record and the first Rupe Tall Trophy. [Rupert Tall was an Invercargill motorcycle dealer and rider. This was a Southland Motorcycle Club award.]

The Indian was getting faster and faster. Each time I went out to the beach it would blow up. The main cause of trouble was lack of oil for the bearings. It didn't have a modern oiling system. The faster it went, the faster it burned out the big end. I've seen it, like a blast furnace, melt steel rollers and cages into a big lump.

When I was in America in 1956 [Burt's first trip, the 'Year of the Chevrolet'], at an Indian motorcycle drag strip I gravitated to the Indian camp. Several Indian dragsters were in action and I noted a natty little oil pump on their sides. I asked what make they were, and was told they were the regular pump for this model.

'Does it work well?' I asked.

'It works real fine,' was the reply.

'I'd like to get hold of one of those — I've got an Indian at home. It's always blowing up because of lack of oil at the back end.'

The guy invited me out to his place, and I went next day. We searched through his stuff and found one. I brought it home and modified the bike to take it. Since then it's been much more reliable.

I used to ride the Munro Special [the Indian] in hill climbs. I had it in the 1924 Indian frame I brought back from Australia. I kept the old, original frame. In 1955, I decided to build a shell for the Indian. I brought home with me from my trip to England [before the first American trip] aluminium for a shell. I planned to use it at the Christchurch speed trials, where I had been going nearly every year for 22 years.

All these years, different people had been urging me to take the Indian to the Salt Flats in America, but at that time I didn't see any sense in taking it there when I could get good runs on Tram Road, near Christchurch. I took the first shell there once and ran it. It steered real good, though I was blown off into the gravel. I got her back without going into the ditch. I did 161 miles per hour [259 km/h] in what was a one-way trial.

I had difficulty getting into top gear. There wasn't enough room for footwork, so I decided to build another shell. I started on it in 1959 and I built it in three months. After that first run at Christchurch, we couldn't get Tram Road any more, so I made up my mind to go to America with the machine.

IN 1960 AND 1961, I kept developing the Indian, making modifications. Things I did included different designs of pistons and conrods, lowering the frame a little, lengthening it, and shortening the steering head and forks. I made new heads and flywheels before I took the Indian to the Salt, though most of my work at that time was going into the Velocette.

I first made die-cast pistons about 1957. I finally decided sand castings took too much work. I figured that if you could make a die casting, it wouldn't be so much machine work. I was going to town one day to get a chunk of steel to make dies out of when I saw a big lump of tractor axle lying in a gutter. It was about one foot [30.5 cm] long and about three and a half inches [8.9 cm] thick. I picked it up and came straight home and began to make my dies.

When I got it finished, there were 11 parts in it, all filed and shaped by hand. I have been modifying it since. In all, I made three sets of dies — two for the Indian, and one for the Velo. I have modified them so often the first pistons don't look anything like the latest model. In 1966, I made eight for the Indian.

For casting I use a two-gallon [9.1-litre] can with coke in it, an iron pot and a big blow lamp that I borrow. I put the die together. I decide when the metal is the right temperature by the look of it. From when I decide it's hot enough, it's a rush to get it out of the die. I once made two parts and had them running in the engine within 24 hours.

I had been planning to make a dry-sump lubrication system. For this I needed a special flywheel. It took me about ten years before I had the know-how. When I brought the oil pump from my first trip to America, I decided I could make a pair. I made them out of two discs of five-inch [12.7-cm] axle steel. Under a steam hammer in Invercargill, I hammered them out to eight inches [20.3 cm] of about one and three quarter inches [4.5 cm]. I built them completely in my three-and-a-half-inch [8.9-cm] Myford lathe. I had to cut a bit out of the lathe bed with a hacksaw to do it. The only job I did outside was when I hired a lathe to get the crankpin hole located.

Right up to 1962, I used the standard 1920 Indian Scout mainshaft, but until two years ago I used the 1928 Indian one-inch [2.5-cm] crankpin. I have now modified that to take a larger sleeve over it, which gives me a shoulder to stiffen the flywheel assembly.

I make all my own valves, guides, conrods, heads, cams. I made a cylinder completely in my lathe about 1955. Every operation is in the wee lathe. I bought it brand new in 1947. I've worn it out three times tuning the bikes. I've had to put in new parts.

I made the first conrods out of Ford truck axle, then, for the last five years, out of Caterpillar axle. You can't get American Ford axle in New Zealand any more, but you can get American Caterpillar axle. I've tempered them up to 143 tons [145 metric tonnes] tensile strength. I had them tested. Every year, I design the conrods better. It's the same with pistons.

I've made millions of things. I keep improving on parts I've made, or designing something different. This year I've already made the valves slightly larger.

All the time, the capacity of the Indian is getting bigger. The original capacity was 37 cubic inches [606.32 cc]. It was like that for most of its life, as it were. That was the capacity when I broke the New Zealand open road record in 1950 at Aylesbury straight, in Canterbury. I held that record for 12 years. Now the Indian's capacity is 58 cubic inches [950.45 cc], and that lets me compete in the 61 cubic inch [999.61 cc] class for world records.

Chapter 9
THIRD US TRIP, 1959: YEAR OF THE PONTIAC

My third trip to North America was still without the bike. I went over by ocean liner. I wanted to see speed trials and the X-15 rocket plane [the United States Air Force and NASA aircraft that set speed and altitude records]. The main reasons, however, were to see more of Mexico, Canada and the Salt Flats. This was about the time Craig Breedlove made the first of his record attempts there. He was using a three-wheeler at that stage and didn't break any records. Craig couldn't steer the three-wheeler, but reckoned if you aimed straight it would stay straight. However, the slightest breath of wind can blow you off track on the Salt, like wind on a bullet.

When I arrived in San Francisco I booked into a hotel. Then I went out to see the national 20-mile [32.2-km] motorcycle race at the Sacramento state fairground. It was a two-day meeting on a one-mile [1.6-km] dirt track. In earlier years it was held at the Bay Meadows racecourse near San Francisco, and I saw it in 1956.

I booked into a hotel at Sacramento for a week. I paid $2.50 for a grandstand ticket and went to all the big races, and to the practices. Carroll Resweber, America's top racer, was there. He was doing a lap on the dirt at 93 miles per hour [149.7 km/h]. With my one-hundredth-of-a-second watch I was timing Resweber and getting within a few hundredths of a second of the electronic timing.

Going out of the straight at 188 miles per hour [302.6 km/h] and into the bend, the riders managed to get round without killing anybody. No one can hold a candle to the Americans over half-mile [0.8-km] and one-mile [1.6-km] tracks. They are tigerish riders.

After a week in Sacramento, I went for a walk in Stockton Boulevard, looking at old cars. I didn't intend to buy one. In the previous two trips to America I had so many close shaves driving on the right-hand side of the road that I had made up my mind not to buy a car and to stay alive for another year.

I had a good look at them, got a feeling for the prices, and reminded myself I didn't need a car anyway. I was looking the cars over. I walked about three miles [4.8 km], browsing in used-car lots. I came out of the last one and was heading to catch a bus, when an old guy pulled up in an old straight-eight Pontiac. He thought I was the owner of the lot.

'Drive this car. It's a good car,' he said to me.

I was going the same way as the car's direction, so I thought why not. I hopped in. It was a 1948 Pontiac Hydra-Matic. It was the first Hydra-Matic I'd driven. It was a four-speed automatic gearbox. The car had done 70,000 miles [112,654 km] and had had only one owner.

[Hydra-Matic was a pioneer of automatic transmission, and

was first installed in the 1940 Oldsmobile. The 1948 Pontiac straight-eight was the first Pontiac with Hydra-Matic.]

We got up to where the man lived, a trailer town. I said I didn't want to buy it, but if he liked I would give him $40 for it. He said it wasn't half enough, but invited me in for a coffee. We drove to his caravan. It was just like a home, with four rooms. The Pontiac owner gave me coffee and a cookie or two. All the time my mind was going back to the car. He showed me an advertisement he had written out. He was going to sell the car for $75.

I said, 'I'll give you $50.'

He said, 'Okay.'

We went back out and I couldn't see if there was a spare wheel. The seller's daughter at American River had the key we needed. American River [which skirts Sacramento] reminded me of the Waiau River in Southland. The river's water was beautiful and clear.

We were soon at the daughter's home. She had lost the key, so we went back downtown and got a key cut. We opened the boot and there was the spare wheel with a tyre on it.

I stayed to the end of the week, when I went down to the Stockton drag strip, a special motorcycle quarter-mile [0.4-km] drag course. I had a good day there and met several acquaintances. Then I drove down the Imperial Valley [in south-eastern California, bordered by the Colorado River] to the Salton Sea, a salt lake, or small inland sea, near the Mexican border. There I was the hottest I ever felt. Just before I reached the sea I lay in the car with practically nothing on and with my feet out the window.

I reached it about an hour later, about four o'clock. I stripped off and dived in, but had to go deep to strike cooler water. It felt about 120 degrees [about 50 degrees Celsius].

THEN I DROVE DOWN TO Calexico, then across the Mexican border to Mexicali. I spent a week in Mexico, driving about 2000 miles [about 3220 km].

I didn't have a visa. I went to get one. It was $6.80. When I started to pull my money out, it jumped to $13.80. I thought no one was going to get $7 in his back pocket, so I said, 'Forget it.' A Mexican cop stopped me in Mexicali and ordered me out of the country because I didn't have a visa.

Back in Calexico on the California side I was having a cup of coffee in a diner when I met a nice little Mexican girl. She was very pretty, and was dressed in white lace. I took a fancy to her. She had a lot of parcels, as she had come over the border to shop. I offered to carry some of her parcels to the border. We walked to the border gate, and I handed the parcels to her. An American policeman grabbed me and accused me of being in Mexico without a permit. He claimed he saw me coming through the border gate, which, of course, I denied. Eventually they gave me back my passport and let me go.

Finally, I headed back across the border to Tijuana and Rosarito Beach, just to the west, where I stayed a night. I noticed one little shack where two or three women were boiling up something in a big boiler. Next morning, I filled the car with petrol, parked it alongside the petrol station, had a shave, then breakfast. I backed the car out and was just driving onto the main street when two guys with guns grabbed me and directed me to go back. They were Mexican cops who spoke English. They reckoned I had come across the road against the traffic and onto the footpath.

I couldn't grasp what they wanted, and they wouldn't talk to the people from the petrol station. Finally, one jumped in the car and started to drive me to the police station or jail. I kept hammering away at him: 'Go back and ask the guys at the gas station.' The cop just kept saying, 'You drove over the footpath.' Finally, he stopped and looked at my driver's licence. It was issued by the Southland County Council in New Zealand.

Southern California [specifically the Greater Los Angeles area] is known as the Southland, and I think this saved me. New Zealand then had no diplomatic representation in Mexico — it was as if I was in the Soviet Union. The cop said, 'Okay, okay,' and let me go.

Americans told me later in California that Mexican police will arrest you on any trumped-up charge and let you go if you cough up enough money. If they had known I was a foreigner without a visa, I would never have got out.

Back in California I heard a radio warning about going to Mexico at that time. There was a big feast coming up. I was told the women I saw cooking something up were probably brewing booze. Drunken Mexicans were reputed to be trigger-happy and ready to shoot at anything.

--------------------------------35--------------------------------

ON MY RETURN TO CALIFORNIA, I spent two or three days with friends in San Diego, then drove to Los Angeles and spent a week in a hotel. I went to some drag-strip meetings. At one, the guys told me about Max Kelly's twin-engine Triumph drag bike. One night, Kelly was there, and I met him. He didn't have the bike, but invited me to see it at Hermosa Beach next morning.

I planned to visit him, and was at a stop light when I noticed the engine was running a bit roughly, and said to myself, 'Burnt-out exhaust valves.' I had booked out of the hotel, and was to have lunch with my friend Marty [Dickerson], but when I saw Max's dragster I spent three hours talking about the bike and missed the lunch.

I told Marty I thought my engine had burnt valves, and he said, 'We'll whip those out first thing in the morning.' We had the head out, the 16 valves out, and had begun to grind them before people were out of bed.

With a little time before the speed runs at Bonneville, I drove to Yellowstone Park, and the shaking car woke me from sleep about eleven o'clock at night. It was an earthquake. I thought the car was under attack by a grizzly bear. I felt safe in the solid Ponty. Next day I counted seven minor quakes.

———————————⟨35⟩———————————

THE YEAR OF THE PONTIAC — 1959 — was when I called at Bakersfield. For years, I had wanted to see the X-15 rocket plane.

[As of 2015, the X-15 still holds the official world record for the highest speed ever reached by a manned, powered aircraft. Its maximum speed was 4520 mph (7274 km/h, or Mach 6.72). In the interviews Burt was impressed that it weighed 15 tons and carried nine tons of fuel.]

I spent a night at Bakersfield. While I was having breakfast in the morning I read a bit more about the X-15. From what I read, I figured it would be going up that day. Bakersfield had been a great oil centre, and Edwards Air Force Base was only about 70 miles [112.7 km] off the route I would be taking.

I drove along the highway for about an hour and a half. There was a little gas station on the side of the highway and it was very hot — 115 degrees Fahrenheit [46 degrees Celsius] on most days in summer. So I had a Coke and asked the guy if I was near Edwards airbase. He said I was and directed me to go another eight miles [12.9 km].

'I was wondering if I could get in to see the X-15,' I said.

'Yeah, there's a road at the end of the runway where the public go.'

He never told me that the public could go there just once a year.

I was belting along pretty fast in my straight-eight Pontiac when I saw a sign: 'Welcome to Edwards Air Force Base'. The sign had big eagle wings, but I didn't read the bottom line. I was going too fast.

I came to a T-road and saw four or five airmen officers getting into a car 50 yards [45.7 metres] from where I stopped. There were huge buildings nearby. I told the officers I wanted to get to the end of the runways, and they said make right then make left past a certain boulevard.

I drove a mile or two then asked again. Before I got back in the car I heard a terrific double explosion. It seemed to be in a big building. I was standing there, waiting for bodies to come flying out, but just one guy walked out the back and nonchalantly strolled over to another building. Then it struck me that I had heard my first sonic boom from breaking the sound barrier. That day I heard it a dozen times — every few minutes it seemed — but you couldn't see planes in the air.

I drove a mile or two and saw a big round tower with a stairway winding up the outside. I asked a guy who was halfway up where the road at the end of the runways was. He said, 'Just keep going and make a right.' This airbase covers 300,000 acres [121,405 hectares]. It's the second-biggest in the world.

I got along there, and F-105s and F-106s — which can fly at twice the speed of sound — were taking off all the time. I saw two big transport planes go up.

'Hell, this is it,' I thought. 'The X-15 is going up soon.'

Back in San Francisco I had bought a camera. It still had black-and-white film in it. I took the last two photographs of my car, then put the new colour film in. I was sitting in the back of the car with the boot up, trying to read the instructions. There was a noise. I looked up, and a security policeman had arrived in a Ford utility.

'What are you doing here?' he asked me.

'Trying to load this goddamn camera.'

'Will you come with me?'

He looked at me strangely, and I knew that I was in trouble.

He asked me to put a shirt on, and I put on a clean white shirt. Then he ordered me to go with him, my car ahead of his, to police headquarters. I drove back a couple of miles [3.2 km] to the police headquarters. The policeman ordered me to park, and took the keys of my car. I was then taken in to a guy at a desk. There were seven or eight police all around so that if I had made a break they would have been in the road.

As soon as I got in, they took my passport and all my papers, and locked up my car with my suitcase in it. By this time, I was starting to get a bit worried. They took all my particulars.

'What are you doing here?' asked the guy at the desk. He got on the phone. 'Bring that man over here,' I heard — I wasn't so deaf then. So the security police chief there put me in his car and drove me over to a second building.

The second interrogation lasted about three quarters of an hour. They rang here and there checking up on me. They checked everything I told them. Then I was taken to another place and met another fellow. They questioned me for a long time. I was getting very thirsty, but didn't ask them for anything to drink. Then they took me to a Lieutenant-Colonel Terry Thomas. In his building, I saw a drinking fountain and filled my stomach up with about half a gallon.

The lieutenant-colonel asked me more questions. I was standing in front of him.

'Why do you want to see the X-15?'

'I've been reading about it for years, and I've always been interested in things like cars, trains, ships and planes — and motorsickles.'

'I've read about your motorsickle,' the lieutenant-colonel said. He had read about it two years earlier in *Popular Mechanics* magazine. He asked if I read the sign on the way into the base.

'Yes.'

'What did it say?'

'Welcome to Edwards Air Force Base,' I said and spread my arms to show eagle wings.

'Did you read the bottom line?'

'No.'

That line I was going too fast to read I now learned said: 'No cameras permitted on Edwards Air Force Base.'

Finally, the lieutenant-colonel said, 'Munro, we think you are all right.'

He finished by asking if I would like to see the X-15. I had been grilled for about three solid hours.

[Reviewing the notes 45 years after the interviews I wondered whether Burt misrecalled the American officer's name. Terry-Thomas, with a hyphen, was the name of a British comedian and film actor who often played moustache-twirling villains. He died in 1990. Burt didn't follow film actors, however, unless they were motorcycle enthusiasts, and the British Terry-Thomas doesn't appear to have been one.]

The lieutenant-colonel wrote out a chit and told me to give it to the security chief at North American Aviation, the builder of the X-15 [and of many other famous craft including the Mustang, the B-25 bomber, the F-86 Sabre jet fighter and the Space Shuttle. North American is now part of Boeing].

We got into the security cop's car and headed to the other place. By this time, I was more or less a guest, and the security cop treated me more or less as he would an invited visitor. There was a big four-engine jet plane. The cop said it was the first DC-8 to fly, and that all civilian planes were tested at the base for airworthiness. The DC-8 later flew right over our heads. Then we walked right under a B-52 bomber. It had a clamp about 20 feet [6.1 metres] under one wing for holding the X-15. We walked right under and I had a good look at the clamp arrangement.

The cop showed me the different planes as we kept walking.

I saw three that looked all tail and very little body. 'What are those?' I asked.

'I can't mention those — they are top secret.'

A year or two later I saw published in New Zealand pictures of the U-2 plane in which Francis Gary Powers was shot down over the Soviet Union. It was the same as those three.

Finally, we reached the North American Aviation security chief's office. He read the chit, and said he thought there would be a hitch. He gave me a letter to read. It said no person not American-born was permitted to see the X-15 without special permission from the Defense Department, Washington. It was signed 'Eisenhower'.

I said, 'Don't worry a bit. I didn't expect to get within ten miles of the X-15.'

We shook hands and said goodbye, then the cop and I walked over to a building about 50 feet square [15.2 metres square]. On each corner was a big sliding door, wide open. We walked slowly around the building. Right inside, with eight mechanics working on it, was the X-15.

Later, up at Salt Lake, I met Joe Dudek, the chief mechanic on the project, and I worked with him for a week, helping him get a world record on a Triumph Streamliner. We talked about the X-15, and Joe said he was one of the guys working on the X-15 the day I got arrested.

[The Dudek-engineered Triumph Streamliner, ridden by Bill Johnson, in 1966 set a petrol-powered record of 205 mph (329.9 km/h) at the Salt, then, on nitromethane fuel, set a world motorcycle record of 224.57 mph (361.4 km/h) in the streamlined, altered frame/fuel class.]

The cop showed me in the distance three rocket-launching towers. On the way back we saw several fighters land, and the cop told me how the runways are 19 miles [30.6 km] long. Back at my car, he gave me my keys and told me a shorter way to get out of the base.

I left the base on the way to Barstow, and stopped at a diner at a place called Boron for something to eat and drink. The cook in the back of the diner heard me talk about the rocket launchers, and came out. I wondered when the next rockets would go up. The cook said one was launched that morning before I got there. When that happened, a lot of technicians came to the area. The chances were another one would be launched. He brought out a pair of field glasses for me to look through. Seven miles [11.3 km] away I saw a missile ready for launching. It turned out to be a Redstone [a short-range surface-to-surface missile]. I decided to stick around for the rest of the day and work on the car.

At 8.40 p.m. I had eaten and I suddenly heard a roar like about ten express trains roaring up Dee Street [Invercargill's main street]. I looked over and there was a huge cloud of smoke and flame. This roaring noise was a Redstone rocket. It was chained down with three-inch [7.6-cm] chain. They were testing fuel efficiency. It wasn't fired from the ground. It ran for about two minutes then the fuel cut out. What I thought was smoke was clouds of steam driven from rock by the rocket's heat. I was told if you are too close when these rockets go off the sound and vibration can kill you.

I stayed the night, and continued on my way in the morning.

SOON I HEADED FOR SALT Lake, where I was the guest of Captain George Eyston, who was trying for long-distance records in MG Streamliners. Captain Eyston was famous from his runs on the Bonneville Salt Flats in the late 1930s, when he, in the *Thunderbolt*, and John Cobb broke each other's land-speed records. Stirling Moss flew over from Italy and drove an MG Streamliner in one run at 230 miles per hour [370.1 km/h].

I spent a week at Wendover, then the weather deteriorated until I went back to San Francisco to wait until the salt dried. After a few days, Hap Alzina, a big Indian bike dealer, said to me, 'Burt, I heard on TV this morning that they're going to run again tomorrow.'

[When Alzina retired in 1965 after 56 years in the motorcycle business he had a chain of BSA stores. Earlier, from the 1920s to the 1940s, he was a major Indian distributor in the US Western states, selling as much as a fifth of the total output of Indians.]

I checked out of the hotel and drove to Reno. From there I called to the Salt, but the telephone operator told me Captain Eyston had left for Britain that morning. I straight away filled the Pontiac with cans of petrol and headed onto Highway 395. I got 600 miles [965.6 km] before I ran out of fuel on top of a hill. I was able to coast five miles [8 km] to a village. I had done about 19.1 miles per American gallon [about 12.3 litres per 100 km] in the two-ton Ponty.

In a day and a night I drove through some of the loveliest country on Earth. About every hundred miles [160.9 km] I would strike a diner. There was practically no traffic. I went through the Grand Coulee Dam on the Columbia River. A spring run-off was coming down the spillway. It covered about 15 acres [6.1 hectares]. It appeared to be 12 feet to 15 feet deep [3.6 to 4.6 metres]. I went through the powerhouse. Irrigation pumps supplied water to nearby land. Six of the 125,000-horsepower pumps were lifting water 280 feet [85.3 metres] to an old riverbed. The outlets were 12 feet [3.7 metres] in diameter.

I passed Dry Falls on the way to Quincy Flats, where I stayed a night. From there, I headed for Seattle. I stayed at hotels when I could get a bed at a reasonable price, but otherwise slept in the car. I ate at diners, where I paid about a dollar for a meal.

I stopped at a big ski field on top of the Cascade Mountains. [This is a 700-mile (1100-km) range that goes from northern

California to British Columbia.] When I left, in front there was a big logging truck — about 35 tons [31.8 metric tonnes] — and about 100 miles [160.9 km] of downgrades ahead. Right behind was another big truck. They were cruising at 75 miles per hour [120.7 km/h]. I was sandwiched between them in the Ponty. I was amazed the brakes didn't burn out. We slowed, and finally the front guy stopped to unload logs. I hopped out of the Ponty and called out to him, 'How come you don't burn out your brakes?' He explained they were water-cooled.

Washington state is famous for its floating [pontoon] bridges, and I drove over one to Seattle, where I stayed a week. Then I drove to Canada. After visiting Harrison Lakes, I headed for Dawson City, in the Yukon. My dollars were running low, however, and I called off my trip at Kitimat. I returned to the United States, calling at Blaine, on the Canadian border. An American man said to me that a Mrs Munro, a foreign woman, had been visiting that week. She proved to be a lady who sat at my dining table on the voyage to America.

About this time, I had to put two new tyres on the front of the Pontiac. They were practically worn through the tubes. I replaced them with a pair I bought virtually new for $5 for the pair.

I got right down to San Francisco and booked into a hotel for a week before the ship sailed. I had a buyer for the car over in Oakland from three months earlier. I rang him up. I wanted $75, but eventually settled for $52. The day I sold, I had covered 10,000 miles [16,093 km] in it. The only work I did was put in new valves, and I made a $2 profit. It was the best car I had in America. I did some running in it.

From San Francisco, I set off for home by ship. That was 1959, the year of the Pontiac.

Chapter 10
TERETONGA CRASH

[Teretonga Park, just west of Invercargill, is a 1.63-mile (2.62-km), seven-corner racing circuit. Burt Munro's Teretonga crash became legendary among Southland motorcyclists. George Begg, in his book, says Ossie Bulman, on a 350 cc Manx Norton, and Trevor Emerson, on a 350 cc 7R AJS, were challenged by the lightly clothed Burt when he was at Teretonga practising standing quarter-mile sprints on the Velocette. Ossie and Trevor came around a bend heading for the concrete strip about 400 metres (437.4 yards) ahead. They were doing 90 mph (144.8 km/h). Burt swept past them going at least 20 mph (32 km/h) faster when he went into a wobble. Ossie says Burt jumped off just before the bike crashed and leaped 30 feet (9.1 metres) in the air. They found Burt unconscious, covered in blood, clothes in tatters, and his 'pudding basin' crash helmet split. To their relief, after a time Burt regained consciousness, and said, 'I beat you buggers.' He complained his arm hurt, then asked about his bike, which, the pair told him, was scattered over the track. They visited Burt in hospital that night, and he again asked about his bike. Burt's account in the interviews differed in detail from George Begg's account, perhaps because of memory shaken by concussion.]

I was just back from America in 1959, and was working on the Indian one Sunday when some of the motorcycle club boys came around. They were on their way to the Teretonga racing track near Invercargill, and I said I had done a lot of work on the Velocette but hadn't tested it.

'You better come out.'

I said, 'Okay,' and went with them, though I was wearing just a T-shirt, light American slacks and tennis shoes.

We made several runs over the standing quarter at Teretonga, then two of us decided to have a match race. I conceded the other lad, Johnny Young, a second or two start. Going off the concrete, I got into a fast speed wobble — I was doing about 110 miles per hour [177 km/h]. I decided I would never get out of it, so I jumped off the side. The moment I jumped, the bike straightened up. It was still full throttle. Nobody saw where it went. They were too busy watching me skidding, rolling, bouncing. Someone reckoned I went 15 feet [4.6 metres] high in one bounce.

My mate went to take me to the morgue, then saw me get up on my knees. They took me to hospital. My clothing, T-shirt, gloves, everything, was torn to shreds. The waistband of my trousers was about all I had left. Later, Mr and Mrs Stuart Varley, who had been watching from near where I leaped off, told me I stepped off very neatly. My bash hat never hit the ground. I was skinned from hips to ankles. The palms of my hands were scraped through the gloves.

In hospital they stitched me up, and I woke in the morning

bandaged. I stayed in hospital for some time, then had to go there each day for the seven and a half weeks it took the wounds to heal.

I rebuilt the Velocette. I lengthened the frame and made other modifications. As soon as I was fit enough to ride, I took it back to Teretonga and put it over the course full bore to see if the modifications worked. It was much better. I did the run several times, then suddenly it went into a wobble.

I figured later that, as the power increased year by year, the Velocette became a bit light in front. You have to have weight on the front of a bike for it to be effective. The harder the bike pulls, the lighter it gets in front.

I won't race at Teretonga, and I was there when the first races were held. It's too slippery. I would rather ride on a gravel road.

[Interestingly, although Burt regarded the Teretonga circuit as too dangerous to race on, he was happy to do time trials there.]

It took seven and a half weeks to straighten out the Velocette after the Teretonga crash. I was working every day on either the Velo or the Indian, but most of the time on the Velo. [Burt never let injuries interfere with his tinkering.]

I WENT TO BEACH RACES and up to Christchurch for the speed trials a couple of times each year. There were hill climbs, the grand prix at Southbridge, and beach races in Dunedin.

About this time, I made two black flags for the races at Oreti Beach. They were 18 inches [45.7 cm] wide, three feet [0.9 metres] high, and were stitched to two sticks of doweling. They were pushed into the sand on the outer end of the timing clock so the riders could see them plainly from a mile [1.6 km] away, and knew where to aim for. The idea of the thin doweling was it couldn't hurt anyone. They lost all this stuff, and replaced it with similar flags on two-inch by two-inch [5-cm by 5-cm] posts. On a race day when the course was very rough they put one of these flags halfway down the course — in the middle of the mile.

[The flags would have been course markers. Today the Southland Motorcycle Club marks the course with plastic drums filled with water, or road-traffic cones, or stacked tyres.]

I was overtaking two riders fairly close to the flag and had to swoop towards it to miss them. I was doing 128 miles per hour [206 km/h] and my foot hit the post. I thought the foot was shattered, but finished the lap. I did another mile and a half [2.4 km], cursing the nuts who put the two-by-two in the beach. I broke two bones, and my foot was in plaster for a few weeks.

I had an adventure on the Velocette in the mid-1960s. I was running in the Eastern Southland Sports Car Club's standing mile. The course had three bends. On the second, I banked right over, nearly flat. I was doing 128 miles per hour [206 km/h]. I swung about an inch and a half [3.8 cm] to miss a hedgehog. That was just enough to let the Velocette bore off the road into long grass and rocks, some as big as a loaf of bread. I went 80 yards [73.1 metres] like that and never closed the throttle. The broadsiding bike flicked big stones over a fence 50 feet [15.2 metres] away.

I got the bike out of the skid and upright and finished the course with quarter of a bale of grass in the wheels — and with a very sore left foot. The officials offered to run me back in a car or van. I got them to push me off, and I rode back on a detour road, doing up to 80 miles per hour [128.7 km/h] and swinging my foot in the air all the way. I had an oversize joint in that foot for about 15 months.

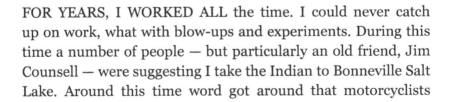

I WAS ALWAYS MAKING AND developing pistons. I made several connecting rods for the Velo. One tempered out at 111 pounds per square inch tensile strength. When I took the conrod made of axle steel to get tested, it cracked and I had to make it again. I kept doing this.

When new, the Velocette would probably have done 75 miles per hour [120.7 km/h]. By the time I bought it for five pounds [$10], the bike had had many owners. The first time I took it to Christchurch it did 102 miles per hour [164.2 km/h]. In Christchurch the next year, 1957, it did 108 miles per hour [173.8 km/h], then 120.81 miles per hour [194.4 km/h], the speed I had done on the Indian 20 years before. In 1959, I did 127.21 miles per hour [204.7 km/h], then at Timaru speed trials 128.58 miles per hour [206.93 km/h], and in 1959, at Oreti Beach, averaged 129.07 miles per hour [207.7 km/h].

In 1961, I did 135.6 miles per hour [218.2 km/h] in a one-way run at Oreti Beach, then in 1965 I got a reading of 138.5 miles per hour [222.9 km/h] in a one-way beach run. This wound the mainshaft out, and I spent weeks rebuilding it.

In one run on the rebuilt Velo I was getting close to the end of the quarter-mile [402 metres] at what appeared to be a record speed when the conrod broke. It shattered the cylinder into big lumps, and one carried on faster than man and bike. The timer ducked as a piece of cylinder nearly hit him.

FOR YEARS, I WORKED ALL the time. I could never catch up on work, what with blow-ups and experiments. During this time a number of people — but particularly an old friend, Jim Counsell — were suggesting I take the Indian to Bonneville Salt Lake. Around this time word got around that motorcyclists would no longer be able to hold speed trials on the long, straight Tram Road, just north of Christchurch. By this time, I had been working on the Indian for 36 years. I just had to get a run somewhere. The Timaru road of choice was too short, and with Oreti Beach you might have to wait years for suitable conditions.

Once at Waikouaiti Beach, north of Dunedin, I was leading in the last lap of a 12-mile [19.3-km] race, and doing at least 110 miles per hour [177 km/h], when I ran into a tongue of water. Though it was only a few inches deep, the splash hit my legs like a bit of timber, ripping my feet off the pegs. From the starting line all they could see was a great cloud of water about 60 feet [18.3 metres] in diameter. It slowed me right down, wetting the wires and slowing the magneto.

From 1955 to 1959, I put in five years designing and hammering out a 10-feet six-inches [3.2-metre] streamliner shell for the Indian. Every day that I could, I got out a hammer and worked with sheets of metal. I hammered out a nose. I eventually took it to Christchurch for a run in May 1960. On the outward run I was blown onto gravel, but the main problem was getting at the gears. It was too tight, with not enough foot room. The shell gave me a run of 161.7 miles per hour [260.2 km/h]. It steered perfectly, but there was no room, so I decided to build another shell. I modified the old one, made a mould, and completed it in fibreglass in three months.

[Burt repeats detail here, perhaps in answer to a question seeking clarification.]

In 1955, I started to buy materials with a view to building the shell. I spent five years building it, and finished it in 1959 with a bit of aluminium I brought back from Britain in 1955. I went in one speed trial at Christchurch, and it took a lot of bother to get the bike into top gear. It steered perfectly except when wind blew me off the gravel. When I made a new streamliner, I adapted the first one for the Velocette.

[Burt has been reported as saying his design for the shell was inspired by goldfish he watched in Queen's Park, Invercargill. He never mentioned that to me, but he did say that, without a wind tunnel, he tested wooden models of shells by attaching them to the door mirrors of his car.]

---------------35---------------

MY FRIENDS KEPT SUGGESTING I go to the Bonneville Salt Flats. I said, 'What's the use of taking an old bike like mine over there?'

Jim said, 'That's why you should take it. How many old bikes do they see over there? They're all big monsters with the latest equipment.'

Others kept telling me the same thing. So, in 1961 [or early 1962 — Burt gave me both dates], I wrote to *American Motorcyclist*, which once printed an article about me. The editor wrote back and said he had been in contact with the American Motorcycle Association and everything would be set for me to run when I got to Bonneville.

The way was paved.

Chapter 11

FOURTH US TRIP, 1962: YEAR OF THE SUPER NASH AND THE FIRST RUNS

In 1962, I sent the Indian off from Bluff in the *Cap Ortegal*. The bike, with my trailer, was packed in a case 12 feet long, three feet wide and two feet deep [3.6 by 0.9 by 0.6 metres]. I think the day the ship left Bluff, I left for Auckland to catch a passenger liner. The *Cap Ortegal* was due in America in plenty of time for me to take the bike to the Salt.

In Los Angeles, I bought a 1946 Super Nash for $50. I prepared it for the trip to the Salt Flats. It had no back seat, so I put a single-bed mattress there.

[George Begg describes the car as a 1940 Nash, but the Nash 600 Super models were in production from 1941 to 1949. It was lighter than the normal models and the 600 came from the Nash claim it could cover 600 miles (965.6 km) on one tank of fuel.]

The *Cap Ortegal* was running late, so I drove 1500 miles [2414 km], including side trips, to Seattle, where the *Cap Ortegal* was due to call first. When I arrived there the ship was due in three days. US Customs wanted me to put up a $10,000 bond so that I wouldn't sell the bike in America. I said, 'I haven't got that kind of money. I've been working on this bike full-time for eight years.'

They gave me a list of lawyers who handled that sort of thing. I looked down the list and decided a guy with a real good Scotch name would probably be the guy to see. I can't remember his name. I finally got an audience with this guy, and so we started on the problem. He started looking in great big books. He asked me questions. One was: 'When you get to the speed trials will you be paid in any way?'

After two hours checking and studying law books he said, 'You know what, Mr Munro, I don't think you've got to pay anything.'

I asked the lawyer to ring the head man at Customs and tell him. Then and there, he got him on the phone and told him what he thought about the matter. He told me, 'Okay, we'll fix it up so you can unload the machine.'

I asked, 'How much do I owe you?'

'You don't owe me a thing. It's been a pleasure to help you out,' was the reply.

ON MAY 19, THE SHIP arrived. I wasn't allowed in the wharf area the day they were unloading. I wanted to see the box come off. Just then, the head man from the shipping company, who had befriended me by then, drove up, and told off the guy for not letting me in. By this time, the bike was in a cargo shed. The shipping company man drove me there.

As soon as I saw the crate, I got a phone book. I couldn't find any Indian motorcycle dealers. There were plenty of others — Honda, BSA, and so on. I settled on the old enemy Harley-Davidson and Otto Drager.

[Drager's was still in business in 2015, just outside Seattle, now specialising in classic motorcycles, cars and trucks, and run by Jeri Drager.]

I went up to the window of Drager's, which was near the World Fair site. For some reason, it was closed and locked up. Disappointed, I was looking at some of the bikes through the window when I spotted a man at one of the counters. He saw me, came over and let me in. I introduced myself, and told him what I was in America for.

'You have come all this way to race at Bonneville?' he said, then took me home to meet his wife and family, and treated me right royally. About eight o'clock he drove me to meet Otto, and Otto and his son [probably Jeri] drove me to the cargo shed in a pick-up with a winch on the back. We got it to his shop about ten o'clock and poked it inside for safety. They hung about, and I asked what was the matter.

Otto said, 'The boy would like to have a look.'

We unscrewed the lid and in five minutes wheeled out the Indian. It spent its first night back in America after 42 years surrounded by Harley-Davidsons. That would never have happened during the 50-year Indian war with Harley-Davidson.

I stayed two or three days with Otto, and got the Indian and the Nash ready for the road. I went to the vehicle authority in Seattle to register the trailer. There was a huddle, and finally a police adviser said I could get a special licence for the state of Washington. That would cost me $10, and another $10 for a licence when I got to Idaho. State licences might cost me $50 by the time I reached the Salt.

The police adviser could see I was worried about all the dollars, and said to me, 'Why don't you take a chance?'

I did, and towed the trailer 2000 miles [about 3220 km]. Cops pulled me up at different times. Most wanted to look at the bike, and some questioned the trailer coupling, but none questioned the trailer registration. It helped that the New Zealand registration sticker on the trailer was the same colour as the California registration ticket.

I loaded plenty of oil into the car. I wanted to miss downtown, so Otto directed me on a route over a hill. He said no hills would stop the car in second gear, but after we left I figured they might.

A HOWLING WESTERLY WAS DRIVING me inland as I crossed the Cascade Mountains. Once I was over them, I was making great time, mostly through forest land. I would have been doing 60 to 65 miles per hour [96.5 to 104.6 km/h]. All of a sudden I heard a nut come loose on a coupling out the back. I thought, 'I'll go a mile or two and see if I can get a place I can pull off the road.' The traffic goes so fast you hate stopping on the road.

Suddenly the car started to duck and dive. I tried to get it, the trailer and the Indian under control. The trailer was out on the end of its chain. Somehow I managed to stay on the road and stop. I locked everything together with my vice-grips [locking pliers]. This held until I reached a gas station. Quite a crowd gathered as I put on a couple of new nuts. People wanted to talk about my 'sickle'. That was what I usually heard it called in America. I continued on my way, putting oil into the Super Nash every hundred miles [160.9 km].

The next breakdown was in Idaho desert country [perhaps the Owyhee Canyonlands, the high desert country of south-west Idaho]. It was hot, and I was belting along. I stopped to put in oil and water. By this time I was getting fast at this routine.

[George Begg explains that the catch on the Nash's hood (bonnet) was broken, and Burt used the oil dipstick to prop it open.]

I forgot about the dipstick and pulled the hood down with a crash. The springs on it were quite weak by this time. Instantly I felt hot water on my legs. When the hood came down the dipstick shot past everything and punched a half-inch [1.27-cm] hole clean through the radiator, four inches [10.16 cm] from the bottom.

I was about 20 miles [32 km] from the nearest town, Mountain Home. There was an air force base a little closer. I could see in the distance an old-time gas station and diner. I thought if I could get there I might be able to patch the car up a bit. I managed to get there without water in the block. I stuffed a rag and wood in the radiator and filled it up. It kept leaking, but not as badly.

I went into the diner for a cup of coffee. A traveller asked if I was having a bit of trouble. I told him the story, and he said, 'You'll never make it to Salt Lake in the mountains and that unless your radiator is fixed.' I said I would have to try after coming so far. He told me there was a man in Mountain Home who fixed radiators.

So I filled all the water cans, and a lady told me there was a little pond a few miles down the road. With all the cans of water, and partly letting the car run dry, I made it to Mountain Home. I found the radiator guy and he agreed to fix it for $4.50. I couldn't believe it. I thought it would cost $25. As I continued, in long climbs in some of the hotter areas I was putting water in every 20 miles [32 km].

I GOT TO THE BONNEVILLE Salt Flats for annual Speed Week [sometimes called Hot Rod Week] with 18 hours to the good. I was the first motorcycle there, though quite a few cars had already arrived. I unloaded everything and got the bike back on the trailer, ready to take out. Then I inspected the Salt. It was in very good order — the best that I had seen it. The water table was 16 inches [40.6 cm] below the surface. In 11 years I have seen the water only twice so far below the surface.

I went out, and it was windy all day. I rode a handling run. Officials asked about the handling of the bike. I said I had never ridden in the new shell except in low gear for about a hundred yards [91.4 metres], and lots of people asked me how fast I was going to go. I told the officials it might weave.

We started the handling run on the warm-up track, and as soon as I started to get going it started to weave and I couldn't stop it. I was belting along at what I found out later was 95 miles per hour [152.9 km/h] with two or three carloads of officials and friends, including Rollie Free and Marty Dickerson, following. I decided to try more throttle in second gear. It sure went fast, but it was still weaving. I turned around and came back the other way. I thought, 'I might as well pack her up and go back to Seattle. They'll never let me run, on account of the danger.'

The American Motorcycle Association's Speed Week steward, Earl Flanders, came over and said, 'It handles quite good, huh.'

I was so surprised. 'Do you think so?'

'My word, when you got to top, you left us standing and we were doing ninety-five.'

I looked at him. 'I was never in top gear. I wasn't even flat in second.'

Rollie Free and others knew I was weaving in the run, and Rollie kept warning me I should go slow. Rollie's own shell had been built by an aerodynamist — Rollie had a sponsor — and he knew what could happen. Rollie had done cautious test runs, getting progressively faster. So I promised I wouldn't go flat out in my qualifying run.

WHILE AT THE SALT FLATS, I kept my bike in Wendover, at the State Line Garage of my friend Howard DeVaney. Howard was a great engineer and very quick on the uptake. At his garage he helped John Cobb in his speed attempts. Howard designed a cam to help the carburettors breathe on Cobb's giant twin-engine car. I was staying in a trailer house with Lester Bolender, who I met on my first visit to the Salt. Lester has been a friend since I met him. For the speed runs, I spent 16 days at a motel closer to the Salt.

An early pilot, Lester at one time flew mail contracts in his own plane. Later, he worked for the US Government, and one job was selecting potential airfield sites. Lester is quite a bit older than me. When he was 12, Lester worked the bellows to check the wind flow over the wings of an aircraft someone had built. It did eventually fly at about 20 feet for 500 feet [6.1 metres high for about 152.4 metres]. In the early days, Lester had a Pierce-Arrow four-cylinder motorcycle.

[It would have been the Pierce Four, made by the Pierce Motorcycle Company, which was reputedly bankrupted by the model after a few hundred had been made. Pierce Motorcycle Company was a subsidiary of the Pierce-Arrow Motor Car Company.]

IN THE RUNS, ROLLIE FREE and Marty Dickerson kept warning me not to go all out. I promised. The day set for the qualifying run, the wind was about eight knots [9.2 mph, or 14.8 km/h]. The steward in charge kept coming over.

'Why don't you get out there?'

'I'm not going out there in that wind,' I would reply.

I told him how I had spent 10 days with the German team at the Salt, and they wouldn't run if the wind was more than 1.5 miles per hour [2.4 km/h].

Anyway, the wind finally dropped that day, Monday 19 August 1962, and late in the afternoon I decided to run.

There was a two-mile [3.2-km] run-in. When I went through the quarter I never saw one disappear so quick, before or since. When my friends found I had done 171.42 miles per hour [275.8 km/h], they thought I broke my promise not to go all out.

'I wasn't going all out,' I told them.

I wasn't worried now. The bike kept weaving hard, but always kept coming back. I was getting more confident. The Salt was hard. I had no worries apart from the weaving. The quarter seemed to be through in a fraction of a second. The referee/steward came up after the run.

'Why don't you have a go at the American record of 140 miles per hour [225.3 km/h]?' he asked. [The official was talking about the 55 cu inch (901.3 cc) streamliner class.]

'Okay,' I said.

'That will be $20.'

Before I could say a word, Rollie Free whipped out $20 and gave it to the official.

[Bonneville records are the average of speeds over two runs. When Burt was riding there, there were three three-mile sections in the speed route on the Salt. The rider's fastest of these three-mile sections in the outward run was averaged with the rider's time over the same three-mile section on the return run. Before being allowed to ride the three flying miles, the competitor had to meet a standard in a qualifying run.]

NEXT MORNING, I WENT OUT after checking the bike and

trying to get more oil in. She was running awful hot. I discovered later that the Indian pump I fitted wasn't too good at high altitude.

[The altitude of the Bonneville Salt Flats is 4219 feet, or 1286 metres.]

I took off and kept weaving all the way. I averaged 179 miles per hour [288.1 km/h]. They complained about the speed being so high without proper testing. My official speed was 179.372 miles per hour [288.671 km/h] in the outward timing mile [1.6 km] of the 11 miles [17.7 km]. For the first run, they timed over three miles [4.8 km], the best mile counting. The course is usually nine miles [14.48 km], but this year the Salt was so dry it was 11 miles [17.70 km].

I stopped about what I thought was the seventh mile, after I was through the timing bit, thinking I was at the end. We were preparing for a return run within 20 minutes. I thought my plugs were wet. I was stopped in the salt desert. Two guys came out of nowhere on a motorbike. I told them I had pulled up too soon. I told them I still hadn't been full out. The pair looked at each other.

They pushed me out of the soft salt and back to the nine-mile mark. I gave a little bit too much throttle and, when they let go, spun the wheels and went into a full broadside. I straightened out then went full lock the other way, leaning over and slipping sideways in a two-wheel skid. I got her out of that and covered ground. Rollie Free covered his face with his hands. When he looked again, I was heading away once more.

Suddenly I was at the seven-mile [11.26 km]! I was expecting the two-mile [3.2 km]. I couldn't see the pits and was slowing down till I stalled in top gear. I still had four miles [6.4 km] to get to the course's first three-mile section, so I wound it all on to make sure I got there.

The front tyre expanded with centrifugal force and started to act as an automatic brake against the leaf springs on the front fork. The rubber started to powder off. My pores opened up and the powder went into my body. Trying to cope with the heat, I was wearing just a thin T-shirt and no leathers. [The flecks of rubber also partly clogged his goggles.] I kept it wide open for nine miles [14.48 km]. I had two miles [3.2 km] to stop in and I succeeded. I stopped out of sight, and the team came looking for me. In the car it was 108 degrees Fahrenheit [42.2 degrees Celsius]. The Indian engine burned up. I was going on one cylinder by the time I got to the pit area.

[As Burt told the story, the bike was more important than the man. What happened to him came next.]

When they found me, I was lying on my back peeling burnt skin off my leg and trying to keep cool in the shade of the bike. All they could see was a foot sticking out over the bike. A 60-square-inch [387-square-cm] patch of my left leg was burned by heat from both exhausts. The heat softened plastic tubing, and then alcohol fuel poured over the leg. The pain wasn't great. They were waiting for me at the first-aid post and dressed my leg, and said I would have to go to a doctor later.

The chief time keeper came over. 'I'm sorry, Burt, but you did your best run on the return on the wrong mile.'

They timed me at 178.571 miles per hour [287.38 km/h] but for the same — final — section on the return run I had blown the piston and was slowing down. The rules say you have to use the same mile in each run. The third of the three they measured was about 145 miles per hour [233.3 km/h]. This gave me an average of 162 miles per hour [260.7 km/h].

[George Begg confirms that Burt's first mile was his best on the outward run, but the third mile on the return run, against which it had to be averaged for the record bid, was well down.]

I WENT BACK TO HOWARD DeVaney's workshop in Wendover and for two days worked day and night. I was finding why the pump wasn't working, grinding valves, and fixing the broken clutch lever. I was also dressing my leg, which was starting to get painful.

I was out the garage door ready to go back to the Salt when a couple of nice women arrived at the door. They said they had been looking everywhere for me. They asked if I would come to the caravan at the Salt Flat and have a drink with them. When I got there, Lester Nehamkin, a well-known photographer, poured me a drink and boy could I go it. It was hot and dry. Lester said that every year the Speed Week committee awarded a trophy for Sportsman of the Year. There was a meeting the night before, and I was elected.

'Would you bring your sickle down to the starting line? We're having a presentation.'

I was thunderstruck. I hauled down there with several record breakers, including the man with a 2623 cc Harley-Davidson. They made speeches and took a lot of photographs, and presented me with a bag of dollars. I was privileged to kiss the trophy girls, and one took a bit of catching. Then a guy wanted to buy my cams and offered me $350, which I took smartly. I finished up with a lot of dollars — $1320 altogether — which I banked for a new car. Even after the presentation, people were stopping me and offering money to help me on my way.

I bogged in and worked on the bike. I went out to try to get to qualify and get two good runs together, and I melted a piston again.

After the presentation on Wednesday 22 August, I qualified again with a 175.75 miles per hour [282.84 km/h] six-mile run. I went out again on the Thursday on two miles east and two miles west, and I think I had one run, and on the return couldn't get going because she had holed a piston.

I went back and fitted another piston for the Saturday morning. I failed to get going because I burned a piston on the return run.

By this time my leg was starting to get so painful I couldn't do any more. I ran a total of 53 miles [85.3 km] on the Salt. The longest run was the very first one, of 11 miles [17.7 km].

<hr />

35

I KEPT AROUND THE SALT for six weeks. I could stay out of bed only three hours a day. The rest of the time I relaxed in Lester's trailer house. After several weeks, I had replaced the triple fin on the streamliner with a single fin. I planned to do the first trial with the new stabiliser fin on a Wednesday night. The leg was still bad, but it had improved a little. This was about six weeks after the first run. I just had to get a run. The idea was to see if the single fin would improve the steering.

There were two guys from New York and Howard DeVaney, and there were two or three car-loads of people at the three-mile [4.83 km] marker. They pushed me off, and I took off. I ran her up to about 160 miles per hour [257.5 km/h]. The stabiliser made no difference. When I got her stopped, around about the three-mile, we found she had been spinning the wheel and leaving a black rubber track on the dry salt. I said to Howard, 'Look at the damn thing, spinning the wheel at 160. I think it might be causing the weaving. I'll fix it. I'll build a lead brick and put it in front of the back wheel to stop the spinning.'

So I spent two days welding up a steel mould that would fit in the space in the frame in front of the back wheel. Then I broke up 22 old batteries. With the metal out of them I built a lead brick 66 pounds [29.9 kg] in weight, and 4.5 inches wide, 14 inches long and 2.5 inches thick [11.4 by 35.6 by 6.4 cm]. I screwed this in place. It had two wings screwed on so I could haul it out.

They all kept asking me when I would be going out for a test run. It was nearly sunset and conditions were perfect on the Salt when we went out. Howard DeVaney, his wife, and the two New Yorkers, and some friends came out.

The moment I got running, the bike went into a violent speed wobble. It was the most terrifying thing in my life. I got to the three-mile mark doing 150 miles per hour [241.4 km/h]. The bike was going over a five-foot [1.5-metre] arc with unbelievable violence. If I hadn't been a tight fit in the shell and hadn't been hanging on like grim death . . . Every yard I expected to die. Still, I kept the throttle open — I was out for a test run — and I remembered what people used to say: If you get into a wobble, open the throttle.

I didn't think I would come out alive. In a desperate effort I kept her wide open for a mile and a half [2.4 km]. Then I slowed and got her stopped. I even had the lead brick out when about five car-loads of people arrived to see how things were going. They asked a lot of questions. Some of them were from an airbase. An officer among them asked how I got the bike stopped.

'When I found I was still living I slowed to about 100 miles per hour [160.9 km/h] then sat up. As soon as I sat up it went straight like that,' I said as I demonstrated with my hands.

'Yah,' said the officer. 'When you sat up you shifted the centre of pressure back and that made it go straight.'

That was the answer! Before I stopped I knew the lead brick caused the problem, but didn't know why. Someone souvenired the lead brick, and as far as I know it's still around Wendover.

'Why didn't I bring my movie camera?' said Howard DeVaney.

'Would you like me to do it again?' I quipped.

'Would you?'

'Not for a million dollars until I do something about it.'

I went to a doctor about my leg, and he told me it was cooked for a depth of about an inch [2.5 cm]. Two months later it started to form scabs, and I knew it would heal.

---------------------------------(35)---------------------------------

AFTER THE RUNS AT THE Salt I loaded the bike and everything ready to return to New Zealand. I completely rebuilt the gearbox of the Nash in Wendover. The Nash had been through several blow-ups. I loaded up with alcohol fuel for other bikes until I had 30 gallons [113.6 litres] of the stuff. 'I can't waste that,' I thought. 'I'll burn it in the car.'

I finally left, and the first day I drove up to the Washington state town of Vancouver [as opposed to Canada's Vancouver]. Then I drove back to Seattle. At Otto Drager's I packed the bike and the gear, including most of my tools, then got them on the ship.

Finally, I left for California. On the first day, I drove to Washington's Vancouver, on the north of the Columbia River. I had breakfast there and set sail for San Francisco. By this time the greatest storm ever known on the Pacific coast of the United States was raging. The wind was gusting to 130 miles per hour [209.2 km/h] on the Columbia River bridge at Portland, on Oregon's border just across from Washington's Vancouver. I battled on all day till dark. The Nash nearly lay down and died in the headwind. Forty-one people were killed in the storm that day. I never saw such rain. It must have been going horizontal at times.

Every hundred miles [160.9 km], I would have to drain the nitro the other riders at Bonneville had given me. I was putting in about two gallons of nitro to 12 or 14 of regular gas [7.6 litres of nitro to 45.4 or 53 litres of petrol]. The nitro was accumulating in the bottom of the gas tank, blocking the fuel. I had a big bottle I connected to the fuel line. I would hook up a pipe to the bottle, start the engine, pour petrol into the carburettor to keep it going, and she would pump the stuff out of the bottom of the tank until it filled the bottle.

For lunch, I pulled off the freeway at Roseburg, in southern Oregon. While I was there, three people who couldn't see for rain drove off the road into bush and were killed. After lunch, they told me I was on the right road, and I took off in low gear. Then it wouldn't go into second gear. The back wheels locked, and stalled the engine. I couldn't get out of the car because of the heavy rain. I decided to see if I could start her with the clutch out. I managed to get her into reverse, and backed down to the shop where I had asked if I was on the right road.

I couldn't get out, so I sat in the car, lifted the mat and a bit of flooring and took the top off the gearbox. I mucked around, then put the lid back on thinking I might as well try it again. I tried her, and away the Nash went. I drove through the storm till we got to a north California diner called Little Italy. I was out of the rain, but a hot, dry gale was blowing from the south. Because of the wind, the people running the diner were afraid to go to bed. I had dinner and we talked away. I told them I had been a builder once, and looked around. Then the diner folk finally went to bed. I faced the Nash into the wind and put chocks under the wheels. When I awoke in the morning the wind had dropped considerably, and the diner was still there.

I drove down the Redwood Highway and on to San Francisco. I stayed in a hotel there for a week, then set off for Los Angeles on Highway 33 through oil fields. Two thirds of the way along, I called at a Shell station for a cup of coffee and cookies.

'You have a few oil fields around here,' I said to the man pumping petrol.

'My company has 900 pumps around here. They are in the hills all around.'

There was a celebration six weeks before, when one of the oldest wells pumped its ninety-three-millionth barrel of oil.

I carried on to Taft, the oil centre of California. I saw them still drilling among thousands of wells. You could see black oil running down through the sand. I saw where a well blew out in 1910. Before they got control of it, for weeks it belched oil at 100,000 barrels a day.

Then I drove on to Los Angeles. A businessman offered me $50 for the Nash.

'What are you going to do with it?' I asked.

'I'm going to put it in my showroom with a placard on it: "This was Burt Munro's car at Bonneville".'

I had got a lot of publicity in California, and the business was cam grinding. Most of the customers were interested in Bonneville. When I returned the next year, I asked him if I could buy back the Nash, but he said he had lent it to some of his friends two or three times, and they liked the car so much they offered him $65. He took it.

It was now time to catch the ship. Some of my friends farewelled me, and I sailed for home.

Chapter 12
FIFTH US TRIP, 1963: YEAR OF THE CHRYSLER

Home in Invercargill I gave talks to a few clubs, and immediately got stuck into improving the bike. I brought the whole bike home to work on: the shell, the frame and the engine.

Sitting home about Christmas, I got a letter from Rollie Free. I made up my mind to go back to the Salt the next year and try again. Another letter arrived when I was having lunch one day. It told me the competitions committee had unanimously given me a record, though the two runs were not in the same mile [of the three-mile sections]. With the letter was a certificate.

I had already put in about two months of solid work for another trip. What you don't start, you don't finish. I had cracked conrods. I made new conrods, pistons, and other things. Making new rockers for the bike was the biggest job. In America, I bought a block of really strong aluminium at a surplus store. The tensile strength was 75,000 pounds per square inch [517 MPa]. I brought this home and from it hand-carved four rockers — overhead valve rockers. It was something strong but not too heavy, and something to help cool the valve.

I had sold the old cams in America, so I made a new set out of axle steel to replace them, then discovered the rocker design upset the valve timing. It put it too far out to be of any use. When I discovered this, I thought, 'I'm not scrapping my new rockers.' I decided to have a go at making the bike into a four-cam Indian instead of a two-cam Indian. This entailed trial and error over about 800 hours of work. It meant making 17 cam followers, cut out by hand with a narrow hacksaw blade. I made 14, and a very large number of eccentric tappet guides to work in the four cams. This entailed junking out all the bronze fittings in the timing case and replacing them with needle rollers. I finally got it working, and it worked very well on my next visit to the Salt.

I raised the back part of the frame an inch [2.5 cm] to get more clearance for the shell and put about 36 pounds [16.3 kg] of sheet lead on the front. I made a single large stabiliser for the back instead of the three, which some Americans at the Salt said caused the weaving in my runs.

At the same time, I continued riding the Velocette in beach races and hill climbs, and I went north with it for the usual two or three events at Dunedin and Timaru. At Long Beach, Dunedin, I won the 500 cc cup with the fastest time of the day, 123.5 miles per hour [198.7 km/h]. It was a short run-in. The race was two ways over less than a quarter-mile [0.4 km].

When the time came for the 1963 trip to America, I had the bike ready, and arranged for it to be shipped. Unfortunately the ship didn't call at Bluff, and I had to rush up to Lyttelton with it. I went ahead in a liner and was in California long before the bike. I arrived in Los Angeles.

THAT YEAR I BOUGHT A 1946 Chrysler Windsor. It was in original condition. It had been sitting on the lawn of the owner, a widow, for two years. She wanted $50 for it. I offered $35, and she took $45.

'What's it like on oil?' I asked her.

'It doesn't use any,' she said.

'Does the radio work?'

'My husband didn't like it, so he disconnected it.'

'How many owners?'

'We were the only owners.'

When I transferred it at the vehicle authority, I found it had had two owners, the original one for four years. That woman told more lies than any man I had to deal with.

Time was running out, and I had to do the car's brakes myself. I finally got it ready and set out for Gustine, about 400 miles [643.7 km] up the highway in mid-California. [More likely, about 270 miles (434.5 km) from Los Angeles.] I didn't get far when I had to drain the oil again and put in a gallon [3.78 litres]. By mid-afternoon, the police pulled me up.

'Look at my windscreen,' the cop said. Droplets of oil dotted it. 'Operating a vehicle that throws out oil is a violation of Californian traffic law.' By this time I had put in about five gallons [18.9 litres] of oil.

'It can't be mine,' I said. 'The lady I just bought the car from said it doesn't burn oil.'

The cop pointed to the exhaust and said, 'The oil's coming right out there.'

I promised to fix the problem in Gustine, and the cop let me go.

There I spent three days under the car. I took out the bearings. I fitted new packings. Then I went right over Grants Pass, Oregon, and, eventually with the bike in tow, covered 1250 miles [2011.6 km] before I put another quart [0.95 litres] of oil into it.

BACK TO WHEN I ARRIVED in California. In Los Angeles, I enquired at the shipping office about the bike, but they didn't know where it was. It cost me a dollar an hour to park the car while I was seeing them. I said to myself, 'There's only one guy in America who will know where it is, and that's Kai Angerman in San Francisco.' He worked for a marine chartering company, and I'd met him several times before, so I went to San Francisco.

Kai said the ship was coming to Eureka from Vancouver and Seattle. So the Indian was running 13 days late. I headed right up to Eureka, about 280 miles [450 km] up the Redwood Highway. I got to Eureka two days before the ship.

I walked into the BSA agency and found it was run by Louis Brero, who was one of the top racing drivers in the United States. He beat Stirling Moss in a race, then he found motorcycles. He built up his own motorcycle shop and goes in for scrambles and that sort of thing. At that time Louis was aged about 23 or 24. I saw him riding, and he's terrific. Louis had read about my Indian, and he said that when the ship arrived he and some friends would help me to unload it.

When the ship arrived, I went aboard and told the officers I needed the bike off quickly. Two of them looked for the bike, but couldn't find it. They got some crew members, and asked the skipper. The hunt went for an hour before they found it. The bike crate was tipped on its side, under about 25 tons of fertiliser. The crate was jammed tight.

After I told off the officers, I soon had a team helping — seamen, my new friends from ashore, and some wharfies [longshoremen, dockers] working to clear the fertiliser. About eight of the wharfies were in a motorcycle club, and helped enthusiastically. We worked together and manhandled the fertiliser in record time. We got the case ashore and over to where we were going to unpack the bike. The side of the packing case was bent, smashed in. The pressure came onto the bike and cracked the shell in two places, across the handlebars and across the tail-fin area.

I told the captain I was going to sue the shipping company for damage to the shell of my bike. He sent two officers to examine it. They came back and said the packing case was okay, and the ship wasn't responsible for the contents of the box. I didn't have time to argue, and said, 'Okay give me the sheet and I'll sign it,' so I could get the hell out of it. I had 900 miles [1448 km] to go to the Salt and only a day or two to get everything ready.

I was awfully worried about the damage, with the bike dented in nearly three inches [7.6 cm] near the handlebars. 'Don't worry,' Louis Brero told me. 'When you get travelling in the hot sun, that fibreglass will come right out to where you moulded it.' By the time I got to the Salt Flats, I was the one who saw two cracks in the shell. The big one in the region of the handlebars was two feet [61 cm] long and the other was a foot [30.5 cm] long. When the scrutineers at the Salt did a safety examination they didn't notice the cracks.

WHEN I WAS READY TO leave Eureka, Louis and his friends said they were going to buy me the best dinner in the city. They took me to a restaurant and insisted I order the most expensive meal. They wouldn't take no for an answer. When I left, three or four of them escorted me the first 10 miles [16 km]. I said goodbye, then headed inland with the bike on the trailer. I had done about a dozen miles [19.3 km], when a cop pulled me up and checked the bike trailer. I got away all right.

I left Reno, Nevada, on the second day, bound for the Salt, and I was belting along at 85 miles per hour [136.8 km/h] with a hot, strong gale behind me. I glanced at the dashboard, and the heat gauge was hard over on maximum. I shot her into neutral and coasted a mile [1.6 km] on the back wind. I don't usually look at the heat dial, so I think I must have smelled something.

The car was still frying hot when I stopped. I had two one-gallon [3.78-litre] jars, but they were empty of water. I was in a desert and the temperature must have been 100 degrees [37.8 degrees Celsius], but in the distance were trees. I walked about two and a half miles [4 km] to them and there was a man with a pump going and hosing a lawn. This would have been the only water for miles around. By the time I got back to the car, I must have been out of it for an hour and a half.

I got the car going and seven miles [11.3 km] down the road I found a diner. There I had lunch, but first a free lemonade — the finest drink of my life. Two men came over, shook my hand, and asked if I was on my way back to Salt Lake. They said they had been there the previous year, 1962.

I carried on to Deeth, Nevada, a semi-ghost town. At an old brick building, a guy was pulled up on a tractor. He knew me, too. He said he wasn't running at the Salt this year, but wished me a good run. I drove on towards the Salt. I think I did the trip over the mountains and desert in about two and a half days. I arrived with just a few hours to spare.

THIS TIME, THE BIKE BLEW up at the end of the first mile. Too much was gone. I couldn't rebuild her there. I would have to do it at home. It was the fastest I had gone. I averaged 184 miles per hour [296.1 km/h] in the mile. They calculated I was going 195 miles per hour [313.8 km/h] at the end. For the Salt run, I put two lead blocks on the handlebars. This helped the bike to steer well.

When the engine blew up I was going straight. When it blew,

the conrod hammered the piston. It shattered the alloy barrel, and a lump of metal hit me on the leg and chipped a bone in the knee. I got her stopped in three and a half miles [5.6 km], letting her coast with my foot on the clutch. My knee was badly bruised, and painful for a couple of days. I bound it up. I had chipped bones in knees and elbows several times on the old Rugby Park speedway in Invercargill.

However, I soon had to go to Salt Lake City for an operation on my lip, which had grown a thing that wouldn't heal up. I stored the bike with friends in Grantsville [close to Salt Lake City], and went tripping for 7000 miles [11,265 km]. I went to Austin, Nevada, and had a look at the old silver mines. I also drove to Lake Tahoe, an alpine lake, and I visited old friends. Finally, I decided to go back to Los Angeles, with the bike engine, and take it home with me in the ship.

AS I FINALLY LEFT THE Salt Lake for home I had a fair bit of water with me. It was awful hot weather and I had a long mountain to climb. The Chrysler got hotter and weaker and weaker until it wouldn't go another yard for lack of water. It stopped within 200 yards [183 metres] of where the Nash cracked up the year before. I watched for my chance with traffic, and let her run downhill backwards a bit. When I got enough way on, I whipped the lock around and shot the back of the car up the embankment.

I made a mistake: it was a fuel blockage, and not water. I coasted down the long hill for several miles till I got to the flat again. Then I worked on the car for two or three hours. The fuel lines were the trouble. The fuel-pump diaphragm had busted as well as the pipeline. I was about 30 miles [48.3 km] from Wendover. The car boot was open. In it was a red box. A jeep went by, then turned back. It was a Federal Aviation

Administration man touring mountain beacons. He recognised my red box from the Salt, and he knew I had left for home. He towed me back to Wendover.

I fitted another fuel pump, cleared the pipes, got a spare pump and set off again on the 1150 miles [1850 km] to San Francisco and Los Angeles. I drove about 200 miles [322 km] to Battle Mountain.

[Burt's memory was fairly sound; an internet source puts the distance at 179.2 miles. Perhaps the road has been improved.]

There I had lunch. When I came back to the car, it wouldn't start because of lack of petrol. The second pump had cut out. I got stuck in and installed the third pump. It was pretty hot there. When I was ready to start, I got a guy to work the starter while I poured a bit of juice into the carburettor. So I got cracking again, and she kept going all that day.

I pulled in at Fernley, nearly 400 miles [643.7 km, but 365.5 miles or 588.21 km in 2015, according to the internet] from where I started. There was always a petrol price war on, and I stopped for cheap gas. When I went to leave, the starter button had cracked up. The gas-station man started it for me, short-circuiting it with a screwdriver. Then I noticed the generator had burned up.

I reached Reno when it was getting dark. I slipped through Reno on dim lights, trying to save the battery and looking for a downhill slope so I could start next morning. It was a Friday night, a bad time for traffic as people poured out from San Francisco to gamble at Reno over the weekend. I went 60 miles [96.6 km] on dim lights, and never found a downhill. Finally I put up at Soda Springs, California, 60 miles [96.56 km] into the mountains from Reno.

Over breakfast I met two construction workers with a utility. They were ready to head for work on a new highway. They pushed me off in the utility. I was on a beautiful four-lane highway. It was 80 miles [128.7 km; in 2015 it's about 75 miles, or 120.7 km]. I got 20 miles [32.2 km] past Sacramento when a cop followed me for several miles. He thought I was drunk. I slowed to about 50 or 60 miles per hour [80.5 to 96.6 km/h]. When the cop ordered me to stop and I pulled up, I switched the motor off without thinking.

The cop looked at me pretty closely and asked for my licence. He wanted to know why I was wobbling about the highway so much. I explained I was keeping to the right edge of the concrete, looking for a garage where I could get the battery charged. 'When I get on the edge of the concrete, the shoulder makes it wiggle a bit, and that's the reason for the wobble,' I told him. He turned out to be a real fine fellow, about retiring age, in a brand-new automobile. I asked for a push start. He said that was against the rules of the Highway Patrol, but he could take me to a gas station three miles [4.8 km] down the highway. I said, 'That's a lot more dollars.' The cop took me down to the gas station, and ordered a man there to get me going, then drove away.

'Where's your car?'

'Three and a half miles back on the freeway.'

'I've got no transportation. I can't do anything for you.'

An old man piped up. 'I'm going back that way. I'll give him a lift.'

He ran me right back. He got on an overpass and took me to the Chrysler, then got in behind the car and pushed me off. I headed for Stockton. I thought, 'If I can get to the place there of my old friend, Joe Simpson, I will be right.'

[Simpson, with Rollie Free and Marty Dickerson, was one of the top three American motorcycle record breakers at Bonneville in the 1950s. Riding a Vincent Black Lightning, he broke Rollie Free's national speed record in 1953.]

I got to Joe's, and while he went for a battery charger I kept the motor running. We charged the battery overnight, and in the morning I left for Gustine, then on to San Francisco, where I spent two days before heading south to Los Angeles.

I fitted another generator in the Chrysler. It didn't work. I went back to the original generator, and found it just needed new brushes. I fixed it.

I had to go back to Salt Lake to collect the bike. I passed through San Francisco again, and on the way called on Bob Wells, who had bought my first American car from me before I went home about six years earlier. Bob was manager of a firm that sold all trade-ins for Chevrolets in Oakland.

'You can't go to Salt Lake on those bald tyres,' Bob growled, and ordered me to take the new tyres off a smashed-up Buick. I took the five new tyres, but had to get wider wheel rims. Later, before I left America, I had no trouble selling the Chrysler with its new tyres and the engine and everything in good shape. I made a profit of maybe $10 out of it.

I picked up the bike and left it in good hands while I brought the engine home. I spent a week or two at the Hawthorn Hotel until the ship sailed. I visited friends, and went to a drag strip. Two or three friends, including Marty Dickerson and Rollie Free, took me to the ship. I had already decided I would return to Salt Lake the next year.

Chapter 13
SIXTH US TRIP, 1964: YEAR OF THE FORD

On my return home, I worked 2000 hours on the Indian. I welded her up, made new connecting rods, half a dozen new pistons, and repaired all the damaged parts in the timing case.

This was the year I was tempering the connecting rods. I went to Melhop's [an Invercargill engineering firm] to use the cyanide bath. I heated the rods to 960 degrees Fahrenheit [515.6 degrees Celsius]. I hard-tempered the rods in red-hot cyanide [molten cyanide salt].

I put them down on the side of the furnace while I put a spare rod in and timed it to see how long it would take to change to straw colour. I put it in for 14 seconds and it was still bright instead of straw colour. I took it out, and washed all the cyanide off it.

I came back to the bath. The rod was still wet, but I thought the heat would soon vaporise off the water when I put the rod in. I had it on wire for testing, ready for the colour change. I would say there was 50 to 60 pounds [22.7 to 27.2 kg] of cyanide salt in the electrically heated carborundum crucible.

I just dumped the thing into it, water and all. There was a terrific explosion. Molten cyanide shot out like a shot from a cannon. It hit the ceiling and came down on top of me. I was in a six-foot [1.8-metre] area of this molten stuff. It set fire to my clothing and came down on my bare head, taking the hair off and burning the scalp. It was a cold day, and I had my overcoat on. It saved me. My overcoat, shoes and suit were destroyed. The conrods sitting there went from cold to purple.

The moment the cyanide hit my head I felt the pain. I started scraping the stuff off and ran to the water tap. Melhop's staff grabbed me and rushed me to hospital. After my hair grew again, a lot of people reckoned I had more hair than before. I reckoned I would start a cyanide cure for baldness, but I never could get any customers. Since then, I've never had an overcoat.

[In 2015, the old Southland engineering firm of Melhop's has long gone. The cyanide bath that Burt used is at the firm which evolved from it — McLeay Precision Engineering. Wayne Affleck, the managing director, says the basic treatment is to submerge metal in cyanide salt heated to 900 degrees Celsius. The result is steel with extremely high carbon content.]

I MADE A LOT OF spare parts. I made all new valves. The old ones were damaged when the bike blew up. I made new cylinders, and made them a bit bigger. I increased the Indian engine capacity to 53.5 cubic inches [876.7 cc]. I fitted the engine into the Velocette for testing [the frame was left behind in America].

Meanwhile, I blew the Velocette up several times as usual. I broke pistons and conrods and bent valves. I think that was the year I wound the mainshaft out of the flywheel when I was doing 138 miles per hour [222.1 km/h]. That was the fastest I ever did on the Velocette. The torque was great enough to wind the mainshaft out of the flywheel. This was at Otaitai Beach [1.86 miles (3km) from Riverton and 18.64 miles (30 km) from Invercargill].

I worked on the two bikes right until it was time to leave for the United States again. I completely overhauled the Indian clutch and figured it would hold all right. I made a special new three-tooth sprocket that would gear her up about 2.5 to 1. Then I set off to the United States with the engine.

IN LOS ANGELES, THEY WERE going to give me back the Chrysler for nothing, but the new Buick tyres had been swiped, so I bought a six-cylinder 1955 Ford for under $100. It was quite a powerful job.

I spent several weeks in the Los Angeles area visiting friends, travelling around, and getting the Ford ready for the trip to the Salt. I went to some of the drag-race meetings with friends and saw the eight-mile [12.9-km] national run.

Finally, I set out for Salt Lake about two weeks before Hot Rod Week. I was headed for Grantsville, where I had left the bike without the engine. About 100 miles [160.9 km] from Los Angeles, I had breakfast. I planned to make it a two-day trip, but the Ford was so fast I soon had covered about 400 miles [643.7 km] in very hot weather. Then I smelled the engine burning.

I used all the spare water to soften the radiator up. The day was getting hotter, and I lifted the bonnet [hood] up. The engine was so hot it was frying. All the packings were bubbling as in a frying pan. I had no water left, and no one would stop. Away in the distance I thought I could see some buildings. Eight miles [12.9 km] away there indeed were buildings.

I knew the engine couldn't get any hotter so I decided to drive along at 28 miles per hour [45 km/h]. When I got to the buildings I was at Coaldale. I had a late lunch. It was two hours before the engine cooled enough to put water in. I started off again, and the Ford began using oil for 1000 miles [1609 km], then returned to normal again.

I carried on and took a wrong turn at Tonopah. I made a right instead of a left and went a mile before I figured out I had made a mistake, and went back. There's a big dry salt lake near there, where sometimes the X-15 lands.

[In the 1960s, Delamar Lake was used as a drop point and emergency landing site for the X-15 rocket plane. The X-15 made an emergency landing on the lake-bed runway there in 1966.]

I kept going and going. It was too early to knock off. The car was going and going. I drove right through to Grantsville, 800 miles [1287.5 km] in a day.

AFTER A FEW WEEKS WORKING on the bike, I headed back to the Salt. It was just flooded with water. It broke my heart. There was water everywhere over the track for miles and miles. It was still wet but they figured it would dry out in time, so I went to Lester Bolender's ranch up in the mountains. He had 75,000 acres [30,351 hectares].

The ranch gets a bit of rain — just enough to keep the trees growing. There are mountain lions. I saw their footprints. I was on my own up there during the week. Lester and his wife would come up at the weekends, and they would cook and Lester would work around the ranch.

The ranch house was an old railway caboose with rooms added to it. It was really nice. You pulled a light cord and it started a generator. Gas powered the refrigerators. Lester had a lot of steel army-surplus huts that he rented out to hunters. Lester told me to keep an eye out for the mountain lions.

It was 95 degrees Fahrenheit [35 degrees Celsius] during the day. At night, I used to get up and watch the traffic on US Route 40 in the distance below. One night I saw a missile go past.

[Route 40 is one of the original 1926 highways that crossed America. It now ends in Utah.]

———————⬤35———————

FINALLY, IT WAS TIME TO go to the lake. That year, the Salt Lake was very rough — so rough and wet there was no running on the Sunday of Speed Week. They figured it might be good enough to run on by the Thursday. Jim Lindsay made a speech to all the Speed Week contestants: 'It doesn't look as if you can run for some days yet, and I want you to decide for yourselves whether you'll run or not.' A lot of people went home.

I finally went out on the Salt on the Thursday. In the pit area, water was right on the surface. I took off in low gear. It was so rough it busted my back — dislocated my spine. I did a whole mile in low gear. I was doing about 40 to 50 miles per hour [64.4 to 80.5 km/h]. I couldn't even change gear on account of the pounding I was taking. It was so bad that several times I was going to turn around. I knew it wasn't quite as rough further on because the chief timekeeper, Otto Crocker, had taken me over it.

At the end of the mile, I was still trying to ride the bike.

I got her into second. It was weaving all over the place. I had to sit up to keep her going straight. I went another mile or so in second gear. I was getting faster and faster. I kept easing the throttle and sitting up to get straight. Still I kept getting faster. Between the four- and five-mile marks I had been a while in top gear, and I was weaving very badly. That was the last timed mile for the qualifying run. I sat up twice in that mile, then leaned down again. The last half-mile I let her weave and kept the throttle wide open. In the last mile I did 184 miles per hour [296 km/h].

The two ambulance men, Jack Purdy and Ted Gillette, were waiting to catch me at the end. Ted had bound me up in the run when I was burnt. 'You were just humming when you went past us,' Ted said. They hadn't seen me weaving from side to side. The rough track hammered the lock nut loose in the first mile. The back wheel was wobbling in the frame because the bearing had come loose. The 60 pounds of air in the tyres [413.7 kPa] helped loosen the nut. The speed wobbling was worse than usual.

I took the bike back, worked on it, and next morning went out for a run at the record. I was sitting on the line, waiting the signal. I would be the last to run. Suddenly, a 70-miles per hour [112.6-km/h] wind blew up. It blew down all the tents and ended the chance of a run. By nine o'clock that night four inches [10.2 cm] of water had blown all over the track for nine miles [14.5 km]. That was the end of the 1964 run. That was August and I left in November.

IN 1959, I ORDERED FROM England special high-speed tyres with virtually no tread. They were guaranteed safe to 175 miles per hour [281.6 km/h]. In 1963, at Salt Lake, I did 195 miles per hour [313.8 km/h] on them, and the officials said that was too fast for the tyres and I wouldn't be allowed to run on them in 1964.

For five weeks while I was preparing the bike for the 1964 run I tried to get tyres in the size I needed that were suitable for higher speed. I couldn't get any. Finally, the American Motorcycle Association officials gave me permission to cut the tread off new road-racing tyres, also with a 175-miles per hour [281.6-km/h] guarantee.

As soon as I got permission I had four tyres shipped up from Los Angeles. I spent a whole day on each one, cutting the rubber off with a butcher's knife and smoothing the tyre with coarse sandpaper. It is now in the AMA rule book that anyone can cut the tread off a racing tyre for high-speed work.

[Tyres, as well as Burt's age, were to be a factor in the AMA finally ending Burt's Salt Lake runs in 1975.]

MY BACK AND NERVES IN my stomach were giving me trouble after the 1964 run. When I got to Eureka to load the bike on the ship for home, I had been in great pain for some weeks. I stayed with Louis Brero and his wife, Diane, for a few days. Diane said I didn't seem well, and I wasn't well. I was getting pains after eating.

Louis said to me on the Monday after I arrived, 'Are you ready?'

'Ready for what?'

'You're going to hospital. We're taking you. We've made an appointment.'

'I don't have the dough,' I said.

'Don't worry about that,' Louis said. 'I'll back you.'

We went to Louis's family doctor. I got X-rayed, there was a bill for $75, and the doctor took off the thing that had grown again on my lip. He put me on injections for 10 days at $7.50 an injection, and medicine cost $12. There was to be an operation next day on the lip. It was going to cost $200. I told the doctor I didn't have that much money.

'But Louis has offered to pay anything,' he said.

'But I want to pay for it,' I told him. 'I will have to forgo it until I get home to New Zealand.'

The doctor made me promise to see a doctor as soon as I arrived home. I did. He and the surgeon and the whole operation, which took a couple of hours, cost me $14. He sent a cutting away, and it was thickening of the skin. A year later, another one grew nearby. I had another operation, but I've had no trouble since.

AFTER I HAD BEEN TO Louis's doctor in Eureka, I drove south to see Marty Dickerson. My back was so sore by this time that I struggled to get there. I couldn't sleep because of the pain. On the second night I got out of bed at 3 a.m. and walked to a hospital three miles [4.8 km] away.

The doctor put me to bed. I was in such pain I was almost helpless. I told the doctor about the terrible ride on the Salt two months earlier. He told me my back was dislocated. The doctor did a chiropractic act on me and got it back in. He said I would feel pain for at least a month, and advised me to take three or four hot baths a day. I did that for a month.

IN LOS ANGELES I GOT rid of the car and boarded the liner. In that 1964 trip to America, I think I did about 6500 miles [10,460 km] in the Ford, sightseeing, before I went north to

Salt Lake. I used to cruise at 95 miles per hour [152.9 km/h] on longer trips.

When I arrived home in New Zealand I found the shipping line had unloaded the bike at Auckland instead of Lyttelton. I had to pay 12 pounds 10 shillings railage [$25], and it took two weeks to get the bike to Invercargill.

Chapter 14
SEVENTH US TRIP, 1965: YEAR OF THE DODGE PANEL VAN

When I came home from the 1964 trip I made two new conrods, six new pistons, and new cylinders. I took the Velocette to the Timaru speed trials. Several riders from Invercargill were there. When my turn came in the flying quarter-mile, I averaged 132.38 miles per hour [213 km/h]. Later the officials came to me. They wanted me to have another go as I was still picking up speed in the quarter. They allowed me to use a little more of the road. So I caned her through the gears and was definitely going faster with the longer run-in.

Right in the middle of the quarter when the revs were over the safety mark, the conrod let go. The result was the worst blow-up I've had of the 62 I've had on the Velocette. The conrod broke. It chopped right round through the crankcase, punched half a dozen holes right through the frame, and went right into the gearbox. It hit the mainshaft, and later it took 10 tons under the press before I got it straightened. The conrod also took a tooth off third gear. Oil went onto the back tyre, and I coasted and braked to a stop. When I looked, I found the gearbox cracked completely around, and the conrod was stuck in the middle of it.

---------------35----------------

IT TOOK ME TWO MONTHS to get the Velocette going. I had to cast a new crankcase. I was getting better and better at casting pistons. One of the tricky jobs with the Velocette was short-stroking it. The original stroke was 96 mm [3.78 inches]. The first time was to about 85 mm [3.35 inches], then in 1966 I shortened it again to 79 mm [3.11 inches]. Each time I did this I made conrods. Flywheels were the trickiest job. I worked on Indian flywheels for years. Over about 20 years I rebalanced and strengthened them. I long-stroked them later.

I had a bad blow-up one day at Otaitai Beach [near Riverton, Southland]. The Indian flywheel was damaged. I bought a dial gauge for the first time, to see if I could get the flywheel true. I worked for 14 days and got it true again.

I decided to have a go at making my own. I built them completely from two solid blocks of axle steel. I got them forged out under a steam hammer to eight-inch [20.3-cm] discs about 1.25 inches [3.17 cm] thick. I brought them home and worked on them for a month. I did everything on my 3.5-inch [8.89-cm] Myford lathe — except when I hired a lathe in town to bore the final two holes in the crank. I used standard Indian Scout mainshafts and a 1928 Super Scout crankpin. I made drill-ways to send the oil into the big-end area, something I had never done before. For years and years, the big end would melt when I got really fast. Sometimes I had to chop parts apart with a cold chisel.

I had the flywheels tested in America on my 1965 visit. They were 160 US tons [145.15 metric tons] tensile strength, compared with the original cast-iron flywheels' approximate 25 tons [22.68 metric tons] tensile.

IN 1965, I TOOK THE whole bike back to the United States. I loaded it aboard the *Cap Colorado* at Bluff. In the meantime, some people had written to me wanting me to bring the bike to them and use their facilities at Lynwood [a city in Los Angeles County] to get ready for the Salt. The owner of the outfit was an old Indian dealer, Shel — Shelford — Thuett [a legendary motorcycle racing tuner]. When I arrived in Los Angeles, I found they had gone to Long Beach and they had the motorcycle in the shipping case ready for me to unpack.

I spent several weeks with Shel, fitting in my new conrods. After I had the engine back together and in the frame, I decided to make another pair of rods with a bigger crankpin. I pulled the engine down to fit the new rods and crankpins and found I had made them too long. So I had to put her together again with the old rods. I did quite a few modifications to the bike that year.

In Los Angeles, I bought for $50 a Dodge panel van, about 1946 or 1948. When I left Lynwood, the Dodge was running pretty rough as I headed up through the Mojave Desert. The Dodge was bad in the differential. I kept putting oil in. The last place before a stretch of 100 miles [160.9 km] without towns was a place called Independence. The van's differential started to howl and howl, and I had no oil left. I thought, 'If I can get to somewhere where I can get oil, it's only 250 miles [402.3 km] to Wendover, next to Salt Lake.' The differential got so bad I had to stop on the beer-can highway [the littered roadside]. The whole back-end housing was smoking.

I had a quart of Castrol R oil, I knew the differential was

shot, and the next town — Ely, Nevada — was about a hundred miles away. So I got a couple of empty beer cans, and with my knife made a filler out of one and an oil container out of the other. It took half an hour to get the oil into the diff. The oil was frying in it. When I went back on the road you could've heard the howling miles away. Later, as it got more populated, I could see people coming out to their ranch gates to see what the noise was. At Ely, I got them to fill the differential with the heaviest transmission oil they had. I made it over the last 120 miles [193 km] to the Salt, still howling.

As soon as I got to Wendover, I unloaded everything and looked round for a crown and bevel [differential gears]. After hunting for half a day, another guy and I tipped a Chrysler on its side in a friend's junk yard. Then I took the van's back axles out — took out the whole assembly. I replaced it with the slightly higher-geared Chrysler crown and bevel. I shimmed up the back wheel bearings at the same time. Dismantling and assembling took two days. As a job on the highway, this would probably have cost me $250.

My friend Howard DeVaney had built a big new garage at Wendover. The year before, he told me his new building would have a special corner for me to work in on the bike when I was in Wendover. I moved into the corner, but so many people came in to ask about the bike, that I asked if I could move into a temporary garage building at the back. Howard agreed, and for the last three years I've been at the Salt I've worked there. The public can't come into it. For sleeping, I made up a bed a guy gave me.

THIS YEAR — 1965 — was the year some friends bought fuel for me. While I was at Lynwood at Shel Thuett's, I mentioned I would like to use alcohol this time at the Salt. They bought five gallons and gave it to me. When I made my first run on it at Salt Lake, the engine got so hot it just burned the pistons up. I rebuilt the engine, fitted the spare pistons in, and got her ready to run again. I went out with the mixture richened and ran again. The pistons burned up again.

I rebuilt the engine a second time with more new pistons. I enriched the mixture again. In this third run attempt I seized up one piston, but managed to get to the other end of the course. I think I averaged 160 miles per hour [257.5 km/h]. I must have qualified in 1965 on just one run.

The bike was now just over 55 cubic inches [901.29 cc], which allowed me to go in the 61 cubic inch class [999.61 cc] for the first time. There was no established American Motorcycle Association record for a 61 cubic inch class streamliner. On an attempt for this class record the next day, the bike blew up and seized. I got to the other end and told the crew the bike had had a seizure. We tested the compression, and I said, 'I doubt if she'll start, but if she does start she'll keep going on one and a half pistons.'

It was getting near the end of Speed Week, and when I got the word to go four of my friends were pushing me. They pushed until I knew they'd drop. She would fire a few bangs, but not enough to get rolling. I decided to give up. It was impossible to get another run in Hot Rod Week that would give me time to rebuild the motor. And by this time I was convinced my fuel had nitro in it. Later I went to Salt Lake City and got a five-gallon [19-litre] can of pure methyl alcohol, which I had used in other years.

It was goodbye to Hot Rod Week, but Walt Arfons had arrived with his rocket car, and Walt said he would give me runs while I was still at Salt Lake.

[Walt Arfons was at the lake that year with his rocket-propelled dragster, *Wingfoot Express*. The previous year, Walt and his brother, Art, in turn broke the world speed record. Then Craig

Breedlove, in his jet-powered *Spirit of America*, took the record. Walt Arfons was at Salt Lake in 1965 in an attempt to regain the record. The *Wingfoot Express* in 1964 was jet propelled. In 1965, *Wingfoot Express*, redesigned, was rocket driven. Walt and Art Arfons were self-taught speed engineers who would have recognised Burt as a kindred spirit. The *New York Times* said in Walt's obituary that he pioneered the use of drogue parachutes as race-car brakes.]

BETWEEN RUNS OF THE *Wingfoot Express*, Walt gave me runs. I recorded speeds of 168.85 miles per hour and 167 miles per hour [271.7 and 268.8 km/h]. I had rebuilt the engine. At the finish, I had to weld the pistons up to get the bike running again. I was there seven weeks.

Walt was having a go at the world land-speed record. The driver was Bob Tatroe, a great American motorcycle all-rounder. The crew would fire six rockets to get the car off the mark, and a few seconds later Bob would fire the main rockets. The rockets would burn for only 14 seconds, with a thrust of 15,000 pounds force [66,723 Newtons]. Bob got to 500 miles per hour [804.6 km/h] on full blast, but then *Wingfoot Express* slowed. The average was just 240 miles per hour [386.2 km/h]. After a few days, Walt Arfons abandoned his record attempt. He took the car back to Ohio to fit longer-burning rockets. Walt figured it could build speed in the first mile and coast through the second mile.

A few days later, Bob and Bill Summers, of California, arrived with their Goldenrod for an attempt on the world record. They were to hold the wheel-driven land-speed record from 1965 to 1991. While I was there it was too wet for them. They had to insulate all the wiring with asbestos string. The Summers brothers came along to where I was working night and day with a box of dates for me. They said it was to keep my strength up. I went home before them.

WHEN I WAS TAKING THE engine to the ship, I was belting along about 65 miles per hour [104.6 km/h] on the Los Angeles freeway to the new harbour at San Pedro. I saw the sign to Long Beach, and out of habit was going to turn off. Suddenly I remembered I was going to San Pedro and swung back out gently. A guy doing at least 80 miles per hour [128.7 km/h] hurtled by blowing his horn. I don't think I've got so close to another car without being hit. There were droves of cars taking people to work. When I got to the cargo shed, I wondered if the car had hit, and there was blue paint right along the side of my van and it was dented in a bit. I hadn't felt it.

I still had to put a couple of webbing straps on the packing case. I had nails, but no hammer. I thought it would be too good to be true if a man there had a hammer, but he did have one and lent it to me. When I took the hammer back, it was still too early to board the ship. I wondered whether the man was the driver who hit the van.

Chapter 15
EIGHTH US TRIP, 1966: YEAR OF THE INTERNATIONAL VAN

I brought home from the 1965 trip the Indian engine and the busted gearbox. I made new cylinders, new pistons and conrods.

[Burt's attention in Invercargill then turned to the Velocette.]

I short-stroked the Velocette and blew it up a dozen times, at Timaru and at the beach.

On the way to Dunedin with the Velocette for the standing quarter-mile, the car went out of control on a bad bend eight miles [12.9 km] from Balclutha. It wrecked the bike and the trailer, which somersaulted over the top. One handlebar of the bike was torn off, and the rev counter was broken. I was able to leave the trailer and bike at an acquaintance's place, and drove on to Dunedin to watch the standing quarter. I was shaken up a bit, and stayed the night in a hotel. I came back the next day, fixed the trailer, and brought it home to Invercargill. I spent weeks rebuilding the Velocette with new barrels, conrods and pistons.

Darrell Packard, a friend from America who had just retired from the air force, came over, and I showed him round a bit. We took the Velocette to the beach for test runs. He pushed me off. I rode about a mile and a half [2.4 km]. She seemed to be running awful fast. I changed down through the gears to turn, and just managed to get round in low. This was all within three or four seconds, and I knew she would blow up. The valve couldn't close quick enough. The run ruined a new valve, wrecked the piston and took a hunk out of the valve seat. This was just one of the blow-ups in the Velocette.

I worked on the Velocette and the Indian non-stop for seven months until I went to America in 1966. Most of the time I was rebuilding the Velo, but for the Indian I did a lot of work on the carburettor, solving the flooding problem. I designed a new big end to take the standard Indian crankpin with a quarter-inch [0.64-cm] sleeve on it. I made eight new pistons and took six with me. In America, I didn't have to put one in. I didn't build a new shell to take with me.

MY FRIEND DUNCAN MEIKLE SAID he needed a holiday and offered to drive me to Auckland in his van. He drove me up, stopping to visit relatives on the way. Duncan had to return to Invercargill for a wedding, and he left Auckland before the ship the *Oriana* sailed for America.

We left Auckland for Vancouver, and I finally arrived at the passenger terminal of the Port of Los Angeles in San Pedro Bay. Two or three friends met me. That was the year that Sam Pierce got me to move the bike to his motorcycle agency at San Gabriel.

Sam got me a late-model, practically new, International van and put it in my name. It was the only vehicle I didn't have to work on for days and days on my American trips. The only job I did was put in an indicator unit.

After all was ready, I visited a friend in Loma Linda, California, for a few days, then decided to go to Mexico to look at a dry lake called Laguna Salada, south-east of Mexicali [the dry lake is in the Sonoran Desert of Baja California, 19 miles (30 km) south-west of Mexicali]. Darrell Packard was with me. I had so much trouble the last time I visited Mexico, I didn't like to go down on my own. On the way down it was very hot: 108 degrees Fahrenheit [42.2 degrees Celsius] on a public thermometer.

We got down to Mexicali and had a good look around trying to find the guy building a speed track on the dry lake. We didn't find him, and couldn't find even which road to take to the lake. We drove back to the US border patrol, and the guy knew right away. We had to take the Tijuana road. We left to head down the highway. What road holes. You could drop a car in them, particularly in the suburbs of Mexicali. The roads were like those in Australia 40 years earlier. By the time we got to the lake it was mid-afternoon and it was 115 degrees Fahrenheit [46.1 degrees Celsius] in the shade. It was too hot to eat, but we drank a couple of beers.

We crossed another range of mountains and found the lake in between two ranges. It was a sea of dust, about 15 miles [24.1 km] wide. Way in the distance we saw a cloud of dust. It was a grader working. I decided to go right out and see the guy. The grader driver turned out to be a Mexican who spoke English. The Mexican didn't know how big the lake was. I sampled the ground and decided it would never be of use to anyone unless under concrete or asphalt. They were building two tracks — a straight one 20 miles [32.2 km] long, and a circular track 25 miles [40.2 km] long. Very ambitious. I wished I could have found the fellow behind it, a Bill Martin. I told the grader driver that Bill Martin was wasting time and money. This would never be anything but dust.

As we left and got back near the road, I saw a station wagon [ranch wagon] come out of the dust. In it were a Mexican and his wife. We both stopped. The husband spoke English. They had a chicken farm with thousands of birds at the other end of the lake. I don't know what he fed them on. He said the dry lake was 35 miles [56.3 km] long.

We headed back to Mexicali the next day, and I tried to find Bill Martin. I never did find him. We then headed north to the border. It was so hot that Darrell started to go out to it in the heat. Back in the United States we rested a while, had cold drinks, and Darrell was soon okay.

I HEADED FOR WENDOVER THROUGH Tonopah, Nevada, one of the great silver-mining areas. I stayed the night at Warm Springs. This is almost rainless country. The winter snow melts and comes out of the mountain warm. I swam in a warm pool. I reached Wendover a week before Hot Rod Week. I had a new bed fixed up in the back of the van, and I slept in the vehicle.

When it came to the week, I was first to run. Bob Higbee, the starter and a veteran of Hot Rod Week since it began, came to me.

'Burt, we're having trouble with the phones. Would you like to go through?'

'You bet,' I said, but the possibility of going through and not getting timed was in my mind. I took it easy and qualified fast enough to have a run at the record.

Next day, I was going at a terrific speed — some said at over 200 miles per hour [321.9 km/h] — when I felt the bike start to go into a speed wobble. It was just before the first timed mile,

I was told later. I knew there was only one way I could control the bike — by sitting up. The moment I lifted my head, the wind tore my goggles off and the wind pressure blinded me. Lifting shifts the centre of gravity back. The bike actually got light in front and I was able to get out of the speed wobble. I had about 36 pounds [16.3 kg] of lead between the axle and the nose.

I slowed down considerably to try to see, but I was still travelling blind. Later, I found it was from wind pressure and from salt getting in my eyes. I had to keep them tight shut. When I tried to open them at various times, all I could see was the glare of whiteness. I ran off the graded track four times. When I felt bumping I pulled her back. You can sort of sense it a bit. I missed a steel post by eight inches [20.3 cm], according to a spectator.

When I figured I must be through the timed mile, I slowed down, but couldn't get the lever to lower the wheels, and I crashed at the end. I split the shell from cockpit to the back. My team of helpers found me four miles [6.4 km] beyond where I needed to have gone.

'It looks as if I've had it. Look at it,' I said to the helpers.

After I decided I couldn't do the return run, I remembered I had some wire in the panel van. We went and got it. Then we all worked to pull the shell together, thumping and heaving. Five pairs of hands got the wire tighter and tighter until the shell closed and we got the strip that holds it together back on. An hour had nearly gone when we got the shell back in place, and the course referee came looking for me.

'What are you doing here?' he said. 'There are bikes all the way back.' He told me I would have to go back and run after the last car.

I didn't tell the referee that I had been out of control, had broken the shell, and had been blinded. If I did, he wouldn't let me run, and I had come 10,000 miles [16,093 km] for this.

We had to go back to the pit. I checked the gas then the tyres to see if they still had 65 pounds [448.2 kPa] of air in them. At last my turn came again. I knew the same was likely to happen again. Speed was causing the wobble.

On the way back, they pushed me off and she fired immediately. I'm building up speed, and at the same speed again I feel her start to weave and a wobble coming on. Before I left on this run, I got Darrell Packard to tighten the strap on my helmet as tight as I could bear it. He tightened till I could barely breathe, but if I had to lift my head, at least my goggles would stay on. I thought, 'This is it!' as the wobble came on, and I lifted my head. The wind ripped my goggles down round my neck.

I had tried to keep the bike as straight as I could, but aimed right to keep her on course just before I lifted my head. By the time I slowed down and tried to find my landing lever for the wheels, my eyes were so hammered by the salt and wind that again I couldn't find it. Suddenly I swerved to the right and crashed, tearing at my arm from the shoulder. It was the most painful injury I have suffered. It took five and a half months before the ligaments started to grow back. The guys tore over and picked me up. Then the panel van arrived, and they loaded the bike into it.

My mean-average speed for the two-way run that year was 168 miles per hour [270.4 km/h].

I WENT BACK AND WORKED for 48 hours, making modifications, trying to make the bike steer better. My shoulder wasn't so painful for the rest of the week, and I could work slowly.

I had a mould and cast two lead bricks. I bolted one on each side of the shell, inside, to keep the front down. I took off the stabiliser, and enlarged it by about a square foot [0.09 square metres]. I fitted it up with fibreglass to reinforce it. Two days later, I melted down the lead from eight batteries. The lead ovals took a long time to fit. I had to chisel and chisel them to fit the contours. I held them on with three bolts on each side, and this brought the centre of gravity to about 33 per cent from the nose. The ideal is about 27 per cent.

Then I got out to the Salt. It was still in good nick. I arrived at 11 a.m. and went straight down to the line. I was shaking all over from the strain. It was a wonder they let me run. However, after modifying the gearbox, this was the first year I hadn't locked in low gear. I have a wee lever on the handlebar to unlock it when I go into second. But this time I pulled the lever when I shouldn't have. I shot out of second and wrecked the cam wheels and timing gear. Broken teeth got among the cams and chunks were broken out of the timing case.

I was 18 days repairing and fitting replacements. I had to send to Los Angeles for some parts. It was two weeks after Hot Rod Week by the time I got her going again after welding up broken parts. I pulled the engine apart and had a look at the big end. On the way down, digging into it, I found the new fork conrod had cracked. I got an electric welder to pull the rod out. I had no spare that year. I worked all one day, welding in the morning and hand dressing it in the afternoon.

THIS YEAR, ART ARFONS, WALT'S brother, was back at Salt Lake with his *Green Monster*. Art had a big team of helpers and a big trailer-truck with the *Green Monster* in it, plus living quarters.

[Powered from 1964 by an F-104 Starfighter jet engine with a four-stage after-burner, the *Green Monster* won the land-speed record three times.]

I had a letter from Art saying he would be happy to give me a run if I ran on Firestone tyres. He duly arrived at Salt Lake, and started test runs while I was still running on my bike.

I was still working on my bike on the eighteenth day. I was nearly ready, but by this time my shoulder was giving me hell, and slowing me down greatly. I finished the work at nine o'clock at night.

For three or four days, Art had been going out and making test runs. He had run at 300 miles per hour [482.8 km/h], 350 miles per hour [563.3 km/h], and 400 miles per hour [643.7 km/h], and then 444 miles per hour [714.5 km/h] on the last day.

I was working this night on a tyre. It leaned with the torque of the engine — it wanted to twist round and round. An official, Bill Summers, came over and said Art Arfons had finished and asked if I wanted to race with Bob Herda next morning. Bob had the world's fastest single-engine car. Bill Summers said the United States Auto Club officials would be leaving at noon but they were going to give Bob and me courtesy runs before they left. So I worked late and got the bike pretty well ready.

I arrived at the Salt about 9 a.m. The officials were waiting for Bob to come. The chief came over to me.

'When can you run?'

'Right now.'

I gave the officials the necessary details for their records, and the officials, including the chief timekeeper and even Art Arfons, went out with me. The Salt was sticky. They lifted my bike up bodily and put it on the track while I put on my gear. The tyre-check men pushed me off. I heard later that Art Arfons helped push, too, and when the bike fired he slipped and cut himself on the hard salt.

As soon as I took off, I knew there was something radically wrong. She was firing terribly on both cylinders. So I caned her in second and put her into top through the miles, and somehow got right to the end. I averaged 75 miles per hour [120.7 km/h]. By this time I had covered six miles [9.65 km]. The officials radioed the man in charge, and he asked whether I wanted another go. 'Tell them I want to have another go,' I replied. I put in new plugs.

Art Arfons came over and said he couldn't push, as he was leaving almost immediately for Ohio. He invited me to run again with him in three weeks. What a great guy.

They pushed me off for the return. I caned her in second all the way. It was misfiring in second, and I averaged 105 miles per hour [168.98 km/h] in second.

[Bob Herda died in a run on the Salt Lake two years later. Just as he pulled up his streamliner car, it burst into flames, apparently from a broken fuel line.]

I LOADED UP NEXT DAY and headed down to Los Angeles, ready to come back to Salt Lake in three weeks. First, I took the magneto apart. The magneto slip ring had smashed to pieces when the bike over-revved. The miracle was how it fired at all. I got a new part, then took it down to Joe Hunt and got him to test it.

[Joe Hunt, a former aircraft mechanic, after World War II developed magnetos for race cars, and then in the 1960s for racing motorcycles. The firm he founded is based in Rancho Cordova, near Sacramento, California. Rancho Cordova is about 386 miles (621 km) from Los Angeles.]

The only part that wasn't perfect was me. On the last day before the deadline, when I either had to head back to the Salt or wait to catch the ship to New Zealand, Rollie Free came out in the evening. I had the bike all ready to go back to Salt Lake, but Rollie said I didn't look well, and I should go home and make sure the bike was right.

I got up early next morning and took the gearbox and engine out of the bike, and packed them for shipment to New Zealand.

I pulled apart the trailer I had and packed all my gear in a big shipping case. The day before the ship left, I had to go to the police court for pulling up on the freeway. I paid a fine of $15 because I couldn't be there for the hearing.

[The interview notes include Burt's suggestion that I use from America's *Motorcyclist* magazine an item reporting Burt was the fastest of the 57 motorcyclists at Bonneville's Speed Week in 1966. The magazine also mentioned the record of 245.667 mph (395.362 km/h) achieved by Bob Leppan riding the Triumph twin-engine Gyronaut X-1. This was the fastest any motorcycle had ever run, but the international motorcycle federation, the Fédération Internationale de Motocyclisme, would not recognise the record. Still, Bob became undoubtedly the world's fastest motorcyclist. The magazine called the Gyronaut X-1 the most exotic racing machine ever produced.

The Gyronaut X-1 was created by Leppan, who was the rider or driver; Alex Tremulis, the designer; and Jim Bruflodt, the mechanic. Alex Tremulis was a brilliant auto and aircraft stylist, who befriended Burt and helped him. Alex designed the futurist Preston Tucker car of 1947. The rear-engine, three-headlight car became the centrepiece of a Francis Coppola film (*Tucker: The Man and His Dream*, 1988). While serving in the US Army Air Corps in the 1940s, Alex worked on a concept which eventually became the Boeing X-20 Dyna-Soar, a re-entry space vehicle that evolved into the Space Shuttle.

The Gyronaut X-1 team and Burt worked next to each other at Bonneville, often sharing tools and manpower. Alex and his wife, Chrisanthie, had Burt as a guest in their home in Ventura, California, on his speed crusades to America. Burt shaved tread off bike tyres on the balcony of the Tremulis apartment. The couple's hospitality typified the generosity that leading American auto people extended to the battler from the South Pacific. Alex died in 1991.]

Chapter 16

NINTH US TRIP, 1967: YEAR OF THE CHEV VAN AND WORK ON THE VELOCETTE

When I got home I discovered I had bent the mainshaft on the timing side. The conrod would never have stood if I had got a fast run. At home I had a run on the Waimatuku road and it broke. The fastest I had done with it was 105 miles per hour [169 km/h]. If I had gone faster it would have torn the engine to pieces. When I got home, I got it ready for test runs, but couldn't get a run until that speed trial run on the Waimatuku road, and that's when the rod finished itself off.

Meanwhile the Velocette competed for my attention. In 1965, I short-stroked it from the original ratio of 89 bore x 96 stroke to 89 bore x 85. A dozen blow-ups followed. In 1965, I decided to short-stroke it to 89 bore x 79 stroke, making it over-square. [A square engine has equal bore and stroke dimensions.] It took 28 days full-time to get it ready to run, including making conrods, casting pistons, then building a bigger carburettor than ever. This took me three months, including testing with a choke diameter of 1.75 inches [4.45 cm]. It wouldn't run over 4000 rpm. I kept modifying the choke until I got it so it would do 8000 rpm.

After the three months, I dropped work on the Velocette to make four new conrods for the Indian, new cylinders, eight new pistons and fix up other troubles. I spent six weeks working on the mainshaft and flywheel assembly. I noticed a slight binding effect in spinning of the engine. I couldn't figure out what it was. Then I split the flywheels and found the timing side had been slightly bent in the bad blow-up at Salt Lake.

I had only three weeks before I went north to catch the liner to America. When I discovered the mainshaft was bent, I decided to try to fit a heavier shaft. The problem was to get a suitable bearing sleeve to fit into the crankcase that would stand up to the strain. I didn't get the flywheels true. I got them within a thousandth of an inch. I figured I could fit a heavier shaft and fit needle rollers. I tried needle rollers from Wellington, then a week before I finished the job I thought a later model — 1928 — complete big assembly would fit. I grabbed it out of the box and it was just the answer when the crankpin had been modified. I copper-plated the big-end sleeves to make an extra-tight fit in the crankcase.

Four hours before I was due to leave Invercargill, I had it ready and running. I was working on the son of a bitch until a few hours before I left. I had put too much work into the Velo, and ran out of time for the Indian.

IN THE 1967 TRIP, I sailed up to Vancouver, then down to Los Angeles, where Darrell Packard, Rollie Free, and Harry Gafner, a retired engineer on the Southern Pacific Railroad, met me. We went out talking and eating for half a day, and I started work next day at Sam Pierce's. I got the Indian engine in and had a test run or two with the new electric starter. I had seven weeks to get ready for Hot Rod Week at Salt Lake.

I decided I would have a go at building a new shell. I had to do something to make the bike go straighter. Then we got word we would have to install a parachute. It was a crazy bloody new scheme for all bikes expected to go over 175 miles per hour [281.6 km/h]. The only way to make the parachute work safely would be to build a shell and incorporate it, then mould it into the new shell and stabiliser. I had to make a release mechanism for the parachute.

Rollie Free bought a parachute and wouldn't tell me how much it cost. It took three weeks to find a parachute three feet [0.9 metres] across. I had no intention of using it unless I was going to die, but I was scared what might happen if I didn't have it fitted right. To fire the chute, I had a control on the handlebars. I had to design special hinges and a trapdoor for release. I settled for steel wire in a pipe up beside the body. Meanwhile, a deputation of riders took the matter up and said there was a possibility the requirement might be dropped at the last minute.

Two or three days before the bike was ready, I acquired a 1952 Chevrolet panel van. I estimated it had done 215,000 miles [346,008 km]. The motor was only fair. It was using a lot of oil. The speedo had wound off six inches [15.2 cm] from the mainshaft. The brakes were good. A friend helped me with work on it.

I went up to Pasadena to get fuel then left next day for Salt Lake. I hoped to be on the short route.

I WAS ON THE GOLDEN State Freeway. After about an hour I decided to pull into a gas station to find out where I was. I pulled off, and the road crossed another road for people going onto the freeway. Just as I was about to cross the road to the gas station, two cars came nipping along, headed for the freeway. I went to pull up to let them go by. I whacked the brake — and the van seemed to go faster. I just missed the first car. I went behind him. The other car nearly hit me.

The gas station was on top of a hill and, except for the pumps, there was gravel all around. I couldn't stop the van. The handbrake was up high, and in the emergency I couldn't find it. I managed to put the van into a sharp turn and, broadsiding in the gravel, slowed her down.

A guy came over from the gas station and asked what happened. Then we carried out tests and found there was no brake fluid left in the master cylinder. During the process of testing it, the oil line to the front and back axles broke. I asked the gas station man if I could borrow welding or soldering plant. He had neither. The nearest place for help was Thousand Oaks, six miles [9.7 km] away.

I would have to go back on the freeway without brakes. I tried repairs with five feet [1.5 metres] of elastic insulating tape. I called a man over to test the brakes gently. When the pressure came on, oil came out through the binding, but there was a slight braking effect. I took the risk and drove to Thousand Oaks. I got there safely, and took the pipeline off and got it welded.

I had friends, the Dickersons, nearby and they said I had no right going to Salt Lake without calling on them. I stayed with them till morning. It wasn't too far from where Marty Dickerson, as an instructor, teaches young Mexicans about internal combustion engines.

I LEFT AT 5.45 A.M. with Marty and we headed back to Los Angeles on the Ventura Freeway. I hoped that if I left at quarter to six in the morning I would miss the police at Palmdale, supposedly the worst place in America for traffic violations [tickets]. I was keen to get going but couldn't find the van keys. Eventually I found them on the carpet — synthetic carpet, the enemy of New Zealand wool.

I knew I would be in desperate straits by the time I got to Palmdale. Soon the traffic was getting really dense. Sure enough, a cop went whooping by, but didn't stop me. I said to myself, 'Thank God', because I was still travelling on a worn master cylinder, too bad to get fixed. I kept going until I was within sight of the Mojave Desert. I was up in the hills and the desert was way out in front of me. At a lookout point, His Nibs, a cop, was sitting there waiting. [His Nibs is an old English expression for a self-important person, typically one who has a modest level of authority.] He flagged me down.

I said to Marty, 'We're in the cart if he tests the brakes.'

The cop looked at the trailer carrying the bike. 'Where's the sticker?'

I had got away for years with just New Zealand licence stickers — or no stickers — for the trailer. I had been questioned, but always got away with it. The same with the driving licence.

'It's in the mail. It hasn't arrived yet,' I told the cop.

He checked everything on the van. He got me to drive and brake. I knew to double pump, and skidded the wheels.

'It's okay, except for the right front tyre. It's bald,' the cop said. I had three spare wheels in the back with tyres, and said I would change it. Then he kept turning over my Invercargill driving licence. 'This licence has expired.' It had, too, in June. Then he whipped out his book and gave me a ticket for not having a New Zealand sticker on the trailer, and for not having a valid Invercargill licence.

Before he wrote out the ticket, I said, 'Give a man a break. I'm a long way from home, and I've been preoccupied preparing for the Salt.' But he turned out to be the worst cop I struck in America. He was out to get the glory star on his lapel. Still, when he gave me the ticket, he said I could drive to Lancaster to get another licence.

On the way, I used the handbrake every time I wanted to slow, both to get used to it, and to save fluid. They had rebuilt the road since I was there last and Palmdale appeared on the opposite side of the road to where I expected. I whacked on the handbrake for a second. It locked the wheels. Unfortunately, there happened to be a cop at the corner. He heard the tyres squealing, looked up, and saw me. I went into a parking area nearby to check up on the van. The cop came up with his book out.

'What have I done?'

'You've braked hard and caused people behind you to slow.'

I told him the change in the road took me unawares. The cop was still thinking about that when two other cops came walking up from another area.

One of them approached, put out his hand to me, and we shook hands. He had stopped me a couple of years before and wanted to know how I was getting on. While the first cop put away his ticket book, the friendly cop introduced me to his colleagues. He remembered my name and where I was from.

LATER, I DROVE TO LANCASTER and looked up Lorrie Edwards, the Honda dealer. He borrowed a van and took me down to the vehicle authority to get my licence. I had to answer about a hundred questions. I filled one side of a two-feet-six-inch [79-cm] sheet of paper with answers to its questions, then discovered they continued on the other side. Lorrie filled my tank with gas and bought me oil, and I set out of town to get to a diner for food.

The first thing they would do in a diner was put a glass of water in front of me. I drank four glasses of water before I gave my order. The only meat on the menu was chili con carne. Hell's teeth, it was the hottest thing I had ever eaten. Then I drove into the dusk and parked for the night somewhere near Piute Peak [in the notes, Burt says Mount Pitney]. I slept in the van.

I knew it was a real oil burner. She once emptied the sump over 45 miles [72.4 km]. I got underneath and tightened everything I could see. The second time I got under, I lost my glasses and couldn't see a bloody thing. I spent a lot of time trying to find the cause of the oil problem. I got as far as Warm Springs, and stayed the night with about 200 miles [321.9 km] to go.

Finally, I arrived at Wendover in the middle of the afternoon. I saw a guy standing and waving at the A1 Café. He had spotted the bike. It turned out to be Frank Hailes, manager of the Chevrolet agency. He took me into the café, and bought me ice cream, cold drinks and coffee. When my friend Howard DeVaney managed the agency back in 1962, he offered to lend me a brand-new Chevrolet. I turned this down, and he offered me a Renault. I didn't take that either.

AT THE SALT FLAT THIS year [1967], I still had a lot of work to do on the parachute. I was making special fittings to make it work when the other guys started to arrive for Hot Rod Week. They were still going crook about needing to have parachutes. They were all warning not ever to let the parachute go, but it had to be in working order. The only rider to let one go accidentally was Johnny Allen. It came adrift itself, shot out and locked the back wheel. The bike crashed out of control. Allen broke some ribs.

[Allen, with his 650 cc Triumph-powered streamliner, in 1956 at the Salt Lake set the world motorcycle speed record at 214.17 mph — 344.67 km/h.]

I was still working on the bike doing various jobs. I bored the moulded container I had made for the chute full of holes so it wouldn't bear down and make the bike light in front. At eleven o'clock on the night before Hot Rod Week started some officials arrived and the whole parachute racket was cancelled. I knocked off work that night as soon as I knew and went out to the Salt in the morning.

I was first away. The weather was very hot, about 110 degrees Fahrenheit [43.3 degrees Celsius]. I had a terrific job getting into top. Finally, I got into top about the three-mile to four-mile mark. With all the effort the engine gradually got hotter, and it seized up in the last mile and nearly locked the back wheel, but then I could feel it tear itself loose. The average in this qualifying run was 184 miles per hour [296.12 km/h].

I went straight back to Wendover and fitted new rings and filed the pistons. I cleaned the barrels out as much as I could. I worked 15 hours right through to get the bike running again. Next morning, I went out to the Salt for a run at the record. I still hadn't finished the work, so I worked another four hours. Then I rushed out to the Salt again, but I was too late. The last record runners had gone, so I couldn't run until qualifying runs started again later in the day. The engine was in such a state, because I didn't have the proper equipment, that the average was only 162 miles per hour [260.7 km/h]. I would have to qualify again.

Frank Hailes, the Chevrolet agency manager, asked me at his place why I didn't use his good hone [perhaps Burt was talking about a fine whetstone or a honing steel]. Frank went over to a drawer, unlocked it, and pulled out a new hone, which he lent to me. I pulled the engine apart again and worked all day. I couldn't get top gear without fluking it.

So I went out again on the Wednesday for a third attempt. In my efforts to get top gear, I was letting the throttle go, and putting the hand down as I tried to get the bike into gear. The engine was going full bore each time I let go, and it bent all the valves.

It was back to the workshop, and I worked all that night and all the next day, Thursday. When the bike bent the valves, the revs went so high the collets came out and gripped the valves. I squared them up, and sweated them in with solder. After two and a half hours of sleep, I got up at 3 a.m. on Friday. I figured the soldering would never hold. I hunted round in the dark for torsion-bar steel. In the darkness, I couldn't find any.

I went to an all-night diner and had breakfast. Dawn was breaking when I sawed steel off a car in a junk pile. Then I made two new collets and deepened the groove on the valve. The whole job took seven hours.

I rushed out to the Salt about 10 a.m. As soon as the record runs were over, I got in the line. I was last to go. I qualified once more — at 190.07 miles per hour [305.88 km/h]. Unbeknown to me — I found out when I got home — a mild seizure damaged the rings on this run. I checked the tappets and so on, and was out early with the other qualifiers for the last half-day.

Because of the seizure I was down about six miles per hour [9.64 km/h], but I still bettered the 61-inch [999.6 cc] record by about 16 miles per hour [25.75 km/h]. It turned out to be the highest record speed of a motorcycle that Hot Rod Week. I got a special trophy for this. There were a record 57 motorcycles at that Speed Week. The overheating was caused by damaged cams from the blow-up in 1966. The valve timing on some opening and closing points was out as much as 25 degrees.

AFTER THE RUN, I WENT visiting round the country for a few days, then I headed down to Loma Linda, the home of my friend Darrell Packard. I spent about three weeks there, strengthening the new shell. I was taken to dinner by several people, and spent an evening at a go-go girl show at Riverside, on the fringe of Los Angeles. I went to the national eight-mile [12.9-km] race on the half-mile [0.8-km] motorcycle speedway. Dan Harvey won a very good race. They were lapping in less than 23 seconds.

The ship was sailing in six days. I had intended to go back to the Salt run with Don Alderson and Bob Herda.

[Don Alderson owned Milodon, which made specialist parts for racing engines, and he made the engine for Bob Herda's streamliner car, which set several records in the 1960s.]

When I found so much wrong with the cams, I decided to try to get back to the Salt Flat the next year and get a good run.

My friends, the 'fan club', came to see me off on the ship. I write to one of them, then the letter gets passed round all of them. They include Rollie Free, who was an Indian motorcycle agent in Indianapolis for 14 years. He drove a race car in the famous Indianapolis race from 1930 to 1934. Later he was a major in the United States Air Force. In the early 1950s, Rollie, backed by a millionaire, ran at Bonneville riding a Black Lightning Vincent. They had a streamliner shell built, but Rollie was the first to run with feet lying straight out behind him, wearing swimming trunks, tennis shoes and a helmet. Rollie got the American 1000 cc record. He made two attempts, in successive years, to break the American 71-inch [180.34 cm] unstreamlined record. The first year he got to 159 miles per hour [255.88 km/h]. The factory sent over special heads and he got the speed up to just over 160 miles per hour [257.49 km/h] for the American unstreamlined under-61-inch record. He still holds this. The last year he ran, the millionaire backer had a shell built for him, and they had the services of an aerodynamist. Rollie was allowed to go up in speed 10 miles per hour [16.1 km/h] after each run. Instruments recorded whether the shell was lifting in front or depressing. Before Rollie got up to higher speeds with it, he suffered from heat prostration, but I think he ran long enough to find that the shell snaked. They wiped the project because of the danger. Rollie is now in Los Angeles for an oil filter firm. He is married, with no children.

Marty Dickerson was another Vincent man. He also attempted records, but in a supercharged class — 61-inch supercharged. With a high boost on his blower in the mid-1950s, he did a run one way of 180 miles per hour [289.62 km/h] riding a supercharged Black Lightning, also in a prone position. He had a special table to lie right out on. The engine with supercharger was developing about 150 horsepower. Marty tried for years to equal that on a two-way run and finally, two years ago, he got a two-way average of 164 miles per hour [263.93 km/h], a record for the 61-inch supercharged bike. Marty is married with three kids. He now owns the Black Lightning — before, the owner was Joe Simpson — and he's fitting a different type of supercharger for new runs.

O.K. Newby, known as 'Okay', came from Arizona each year to the lake. He's 78. When young he managed the Flying Merkel team of 61 cubic inch motorcycle racers. He had raced a world champion roller skater in a big rink, and raced a small car he built.

Sam Pierce, a former Indian agent, has a motorcycle shop where he sells Suzuki, Royal Enfield and other brands — and Indian spares that he buys around the world. Sam started to build about 200 new Indians on classic lines, just to see how they would go. They have four different-capacity motors. Sam raced back in Kansas City many years before. He and Rollie Free at one time worked for the same agent in Kansas City. When Rollie arrived there, Harley-Davidson riders used to beat up Indian riders. Six months after he arrived, no Harley rider would dare stop an Indian rider. That was the end of the Indian war in Kansas City.

Darrell Packard, a former flight engineer on US Air Force bombers, came to New Zealand on a visit in 1965 and stayed five weeks. He then went on to visit an old friend of mine in Australia. Darrell was once tuner for the great Frank du Bois, one of the top track racers in the United States.

Luall Parker manages a company at Commerce City, California, that makes missile parts. He's one of the fan club, but never manages to get out to the Salt. Indian motorcycles are his hobby. He spends all his spare time in his machine shop, and has fitted a four-cylinder car engine, with electric starter and shaft drive, into one of his motorcycles.

Colonel Kafore, from Indianapolis, has come to the Salt over the last five years. For five years he was the mechanic for Rollie Free in car racing, and rode in the car with him in the days when they had car-racing teams of two.

[Burt went to America. He agreed to continue the interviews when he returned. Regretfully, interviews ended rather than went into recess — my fault. I resumed my education, and this soon required taking my family to Christchurch. I never met Burt again, and my grandiose plans, which had expanded to a swathe of motorcycle magazine articles and even a series of them, slipped to the back of my mind. More than 20 years after Burt died, when George Begg sought my notes for his book, I searched high and low without success and wrote them off as gone for good.]

Postscript

In 1967, Burt's mother died, aged 92. In official records and on her tombstone, her Christian names are Lily Agnes, but Burt called her Lillian.

In 1968, Burt was at Bonneville. Weather disrupted Speed Week, but Burt stayed on afterwards and worked in the team of his friend Mickey Thompson, who was attempting records in a hotted-up Ford Mustang. Burt was an official observer for the Thompson runs.

In 1969, mechanical problems beat him in several runs, though he qualified with a run of 191 miles per hour (307.4 km/h). George Begg wrote in his book that it was the first year Burt felt depressed at Bonneville, and he was suffering from angina. I think he developed angina before this. I remember, during my interviews, Burt joking about putting his nitroglycerin pills in the Velocette gas tank. Nitroglycerin pills are used to treat painful angina symptoms.

In 1970, he was back at Bonneville, and Begg reported Burt switched from his traditional methanol fuel to an exotic nitro fuel. Begg suggested this caused mechanical problems with the Indian, and that if he had stuck with methanol Burt might have achieved his dream of 200 miles per hour (321.9 km/h).

Back home, Burt met New Zealand film-makers Roger Donaldson and Mike Smith, who would elevate him from a New Zealand and Bonneville-cognoscenti hero into a world motorcycle legend. In 1971, Burt went to Salt Lake and Smith and Donaldson followed. Burt now encountered the first hint that his half-century odyssey with the Indian Scout was nearing an end.

Burt had highly modified the motorbike into the Munro Special — and that's stretching the meaning of 'modified'. He strove for ever higher speeds in the AMA's 1000 cc streamliner class. In 1971, new requirements were introduced for streamliners. After accidents in 1970, they were required to have insulated firewalls that seal off the rider. Burt had burnt his legs in two early runs and after the second wore flame-proof trousers during record attempts. The streamliner class requirements have been tightened further since then. They now must also have a manually controlled fire extinguisher system. Parachutes are mandatory, and in classes with records over 250 miles per hour (402.33 km/h) two are required. The rider must be held by a seven-point safety harness.

There was no time for Burt to rebuild his streamer shell. However, he was able to strip it off and ride in the class for 1000 cc motorbikes with modified frames. To allow Donaldson and Smith to take video for their documentary on Burt, *Offerings to the God of Speed*, the organisers did allow a demonstration run with the streamliner. George Begg wrote that, without the streamliner shell, the Indian was now hopelessly over-geared. It failed to reach the necessary 160 miles per hour (257.49 km/h) in a qualifying run. It reached only 148.51 miles per hour (239.00 km/h).

Burt left for Los Angeles, and on that trip the incident occurred that was turned into an amusing feature of the film *The World's Fastest Indian*. The axle on the bike trailer broke, and Burt continued with a tree branch in place of a wheel until he found help to load the bike into the back of the station wagon he was driving.

Burt made one more trip to America, in 1975, but not to ride. He had kept two frames for the Indian, one on each side of the Pacific. He took with him in the plane to America an Indian Scout engine he had built from parts over the years. He fitted it in the frame and streamliner he used to leave in America, and sold the machine there. Then he brought the original Indian Scout engine home to New Zealand.

Burt had a small house built for his section in Invercargill, replacing the garage-shack that he had shared with his bikes for so long. He continued working on his Velocette. Burt kept tinkering, though his eyesight was now too weak to read a micrometer, and his health gradually failed.

In April 1977, Burt suffered a stroke. On 19 September 1977, Norman Hayes paid Burt $1300 for the Indian (the original engine in one of the Indian frames) and the 1936 Velocette. They are still on display at the family hardware business in Invercargill. Burt died peacefully on 6 January 1978, aged 78. Norman Hayes' father, Irving, Burt's long-time friend and chief backer, died six weeks later.

As of late 2015, Burt is survived by his four children, June (Mrs Aitken, Waitakere), Margaret (Mrs Popenhagen, Alexandra), Gwen (Mrs Henderson, Whangarei) and John (formerly of Auckland, now of Oamaru). John, at age 81, maintains Munro family ties with Burt's surviving friends, with the revived Indian Motorcycle Company, and with the annual Burt Munro Challenge motorcycle events in Southland. Beryl, Burt's former wife, died in Auckland at the age of 99 in February 2007.

—————————⬤35—————————

BURT DIDN'T BELIEVE IN AN afterlife, but he more or less has one. Burt's legend grew, especially with Roger Donaldson's 2005 feature film, *The World's Fastest Indian*. In Dallas, Texas, Leslie Porterfield and Al Lamb, motorcycle enthusiasts, went together to watch the film. Neither had been to Bonneville, or had thought of going there. Burt's story inspired both of them to go. 'I had been riding since I was sixteen,' Leslie told me. 'I'd heard about Bonneville, but seeing the movie really gave me the push to get up there and try for a record.'

At the Salt Flats in 2007, Leslie crashed on a Suzuki Hayabusa and broke seven ribs. She was helicoptered to Salt Lake City for emergency treatment. She went back. In 2008, Leslie became the first female motorcyclist at Bonneville to do 200 miles per hour (321.87 km/h). 'Over the six years since,

I set my top world record that got me in the *Guinness Book of Records* as the fastest woman in the world on a conventional motorcycle,' she says.

The AMA lists Leslie as holding the 1000 cc production frame and body class record of 200.137 miles per hour (322.089 km/h), set at Bonneville in 2011 on a Honda. Leslie now juggles looking after her young family with running her own used-motorcycle business in Dallas — High Five Cycles. She describes her pre-school twins as being faster-paced than her motorcycle. In 2015, Leslie took them to Bonneville for the first time. Racing on the Salt Flats was rained out, as it had been the previous year.

Many more women are taking up motorcycle racing. This parallels the rise of women riding street motorbikes. This is one of the big changes from Burt's days. Bonneville speed riding is less restrictive than other types of motorcycle racing, Leslie says. 'You can build something completely bizarre off a theory and see if it works. It's a great mechanical challenge. I love that part of it. I love the part behind the scenes, where I'm thinking of everything from creative suspension ideas to aerodynamics, to ways of getting more horsepower, that have never been done before, and being able to use that out there on the Salt. And, of course, there's such a huge rush when you go that fast out there on the Salt to break a world record . . . having a machine that you've spent so much time engineering go out there and do what it's supposed to. There's nowhere like Bonneville in the world. You get people who are passionate and creative, and you learn something.' Burt would surely have agreed.

Al Lamb has also gone on to set records at the Salt. He and Leslie are still team-mates. Al's big Honda dealership in Dallas is a hundred metres from Leslie's business. Al confirms the film inspired him, too, to go to Bonneville. 'Neither one of us had been to Bonneville, or even thought of going to Bonneville. As we walked out to our car Leslie said, "I want to do that." I promptly asked if she was kidding or serious. She said she wanted to do it and I said, "You're frigging nuts!" Well the next season we were at Bonneville. That was 2007. I've been at 16 events at Bonneville since then.'

Both Al and Leslie ride sit-on (standard) motorcycles. The change in streamliner rules that stymied Burt in 1971 made the streamliner class 'basically two-wheel cars', in Al's words. The riders, or drivers, encased almost like plane pilots, now sit or almost lie on their backs in these machines, with their feet forward towards the nose. These two-wheel streamliners are now pushing towards 400 miles per hour (643.74 km/h) at the Salt. As this is written, the main contender of these machines to be the world's fastest seems to be TOP 1 Ack Attack, a twin-engine, turbo-charged beast 20.5 feet (6.2 metres) long. The Suzuki Hayabusa engines' total displacement is 2598 cc. The firewall is supplemented with a halogen fire-control system, and braking includes two parachutes. As of 2015, Ack Attack's fastest one-way run has been 394.084 miles per hour (634.217 km/h). The 'pilot' since 2006 has been Rocky Robinson, as the Ack Attack vies with the BUB Seven Streamliner to be the world's fastest motorcycle. The Ack Attack has broken the world record three times in four years as it tussles with the BUB Seven Streamliner. Behind the Ack Attack is Mike Akatiff, owner of an American avionics company, ACK Technologies.

The machines closest to Burt's that now fly across the Salt Flats are therefore the production bikes, or sit-on machines, with limited streamlining. The rider's body must be visible from the side, except for the wrists and forearms. 'Burt's bike was a sit-up back then,' Al Lamb told me. 'He wasn't strapped in it. He wasn't down inside it.' Al can be watched riding at Bonneville in a good video on YouTube. He rides in 1000 cc capacity classes, as Burt did, and given the streamliner shell changes, his sit-on class is as near as you can get to current comparison with Burt's streamliner class.

Al's two bikes, Dallas Honda CBR1000RRs, are highly

modified Honda CBR1000s. They run under the specification MPS1000BF in the AMA and FIM classes. The classification stands for modified, partly streamlined, 1000 cc, blown, fuel. This reflects the degree of streamlining allowed on sit-on bikes: seat, tail section, and windshield-fairing. 'Blown' means supercharged.

On the machine he calls his 'short bike', Al Lamb holds the record as the fastest AMA/FIM sit-on motorcycle. He hopes to break his own record on his newer, longer bike. 'The goal is to push the record into the 270s (mph — 435 km/h and more). Poor salt-track conditions at Bonneville have frustrated his team's recent attempts, but Al's 2012 record of 262.471 miles per hour (422.406 km/h) gives an idea of the progress in motorbike technology over the nearly half-century since Burt rode at Bonneville.

---------------------------35---------------------------

IN 2006, BURT MUNRO WAS inducted into the American Motorcyclist Association Hall of Fame. Thirty-five years after his death, new Indian motorcycles are on the roads. A series of companies tried to keep the brand alive after Indian Motocycles went bankrupt in 1953. Polaris Industries in 2011 bought Indian Motorcycles (by now the 'r' was in the name), and as this book is written, has models on sale internationally.

Polaris, of Minnesota, a pioneer in snowmobiles, diversified into all-terrain vehicles, military ATVs, and the four-wheel European mini-vehicles called quadricycles. In 1998, Polaris set up Victory Motorcycles to compete with Harley-Davidson in the market for American-style motorbikes. Polaris has been investing in electric vehicles, and in May 2015 bought the electric motorcycle business of Brammo Inc., announcing it planned to make electric motorcycles at its Iowa plant. Another Polaris subsidiary, Global Electric Motorcars, since

1998 has made 50,000 small battery-electric neighbourhood cars. They are slow (25 mph or 40.23 km/h) and have a range of up to 30 miles (48.28 km). In contrast, Polaris is making a fast three-wheel motorcycle, the Slingshot, powered by a 2.4-litre engine.

Burt Munro would have liked the company style. Polaris teams compete in snowmobile and ATV racing, and the firm has developed sports versions of ATVs. The Indian Motorcycle models include a Scout and a Chief, and in 2011 the company produced a Spirit of Munro Streamliner. Polaris is a substantial company. Its 2014 sales were up 19 per cent at US$4.48 billion. On this it made a profit of US$454 million. Polaris's chairman and chief executive, Scott Wine, told shareholders in a Polaris annual report that, riding snowmobiles, he learned early and never forgot 'the throttle is your friend'. He added later that the firm was going into the next financial year 'full throttle'. Burt would have liked Scott Wine.

INVERCARGILL CELEBRATES BURT MUNRO AS a local hero. It's even put up a statue of him racing on his Indian. Each year, in a four-day rally, its Burt Munro Challenge, almost constituting a festival, attracts up to 3000 motorcycle enthusiasts and hundreds of competitors. National beach-racing championships use Burt's test ground, Oreti Beach. National hill-climb titles are raced on Bluff Hill. Speedway racing is held at Oreti Park, including for sidecars. Sprint races are at Teretonga, the scene of Burt's greatest spill and, from 2015, there has been street racing in Invercargill. Supercross riders compete at nearby Winton, then many ride in other events.

The collection of events is sometimes called 'the Burt' — or, as the locals say, 'the Bur-r-r-t' — and, being held in November, sometimes face challenging weather. In the wet, there's the mandatory pilgrimage to the Burt Munro memorabilia at E. Hayes and Sons, the hardware and engineering supplies firm. Here obeisance can be paid to Burt Munro's Indian Scout engine, in one of the two frames used, and also to Burt's Velocette.

As mentioned earlier, Burt used two Indian Scout frames. The first came with his original bike. He brought the second back from Australia in the 1920s. Later, he left one frame in America and one in New Zealand, and took his engine with him across the Pacific. The original frame, which was in the streamliners, with another engine, has been restored in California as the Munro Special, which ran at Salt Lake.

Come a rainy, blowing day and many bike fans will also find interesting Invercargill's Bill Richardson Transport World, said to be the world's biggest private collection of trucks — more than 300 of them. Expect more side attractions for bikers to grow in the southern city — perhaps even a festival of great motorbike movies. An international contest for motorbike videos and photographs would be another consolation for the occasionally rough November weather. Or visiting riders could just ignore the weather, as Burt, tough old Southlander, did.

In November 2015, nearly 38 years after Burt died, I phoned Burt's old friend, Marty Dickerson, in California. It was Marty's eighty-ninth birthday.

'Marty, you and Rollie Free were two of those friends in America who were very good to Burt.'

'Well, he was the kind of guy you wanted to help out any chance you could.'

'Looking back, Marty, how do you see him?'

'Burt was the kind of person you meet only once in a lifetime.'

Records

In November 2015, one of Burt Munro's New Zealand motorcycle records is listed as still unbroken. This is the national flying half-mile 1050 cc beach record, which Burt set on his Indian Munro Special at Oreti Beach in February 1957 at a speed of 131.38 miles per hour (211.435 km/h). The capacity of the Indian at that time is listed as 750 cc.

When George Begg's book was published in 2002, Motorcycling New Zealand (until 1994 called the New Zealand Auto-Cycle Union) had records of seven national records held by Burt. American Motorcyclist Association (formerly the American Motorcycle Association) records set at Bonneville by Burt, all on his Indian Munro Special streamliner, average of two flying one-mile runs, are as follows:

833 cc streamliner — 178.971 miles per hour [288.025 km/h], 20 August 1962

1000 cc streamliner — 168.066 miles per hour [270.476 km/h], 22 August 1966

1000 cc streamliner — 184.710 miles per hour [297.261 km/h], 26 August 1967 (this record was originally listed as 183.586 miles per hour [295.453 km/h] but was increased 47 years later, in 2014, after Burt's son, John Munro, noticed the speed of the two runs had been incorrectly averaged).

Burt's certificates show the record classes as 833 cc SA and 1000 cc SA, but the list posted by the AMA now carries only Burt's 1967 record. It lists this at the correctly averaged speed. The AMA describes the class as S-AF, for streamliners of unlimited design but without turbochargers or superchargers.

Note on sources

This book is sourced straight from the old racehorse's mouth, as it were: from a long series of interviews with Burt Munro in his concrete-block shack in Invercargill. To check facts after finding the notes, I have used the internet and two books: George Begg's *Burt Munro: Indian Legend of Speed* (Begg and Allen, Christchurch, 2002) and Roger Donaldson's *The World's Fastest Indian: Burt Munro — A Scrapbook of His Life* (Random House, Auckland, 2009). Begg, a Southland engineer, motorcyclist and friend of Burt, in his book gives a great look at Burt's gifts as a mechanic. Donaldson, a motorcyclist as well as a leading film director, through his film and print works about Burt, has ensured for the Southlander due and lasting recognition of Burt's great mechanical talent and his courage as a high-speed rider. Another useful book on Burt is Tim Hanna's *One Good Run: The Legend of Burt Munro* (Penguin, Auckland, 2005). To refresh my enthusiasm for the half-century-old interview notes there was Donaldson's 1971 video feature on Burt, *Offerings to the God of Speed*, and, of course Donaldson's 2005 feature film starring Anthony Hopkins, *The World's Fastest Indian*.

Acknowledgements

Thank you to those who helped with photographs: in New Zealand, John Munro, Neville Hayes, David Wethey, Donald Buckley Photographics, Polaris NZ, Bruce Smart, Jude Tewnion, and Ash; in the United States, Richard Menzies and Leslie Porterfield; in Germany, Frank Kletschkus; in the Netherlands, Geert Versleyen, of Yesterday's Antique Motorcycles; in Canada, Cynthia Blackmore, of the Reynolds-Alberta Museum; in England, Pat Clancy and Bill Greenwood, of the Velocette Owners' Club. And for re-assurance it's better late than never — thank you to: Olive; Tom and Amelia; Heloise and Adam.

Index